Profiles in Success

Profiles in Success

Inspiration from Executive Leaders

Volume 2

GORDON J. BERNHARDT, CPA, PFS, CFP®, AIF®

ISBN: 978-0-9972483-9-5

First edition

Gordon Bernhardt conducts interviews of business leaders primarily in the Washington D.C. area who come recommended by their peers. The profiles included in this volume are a result of these interviews. As a result of these additional insights Mr. Bernhardt has published these profiles. Gordon Bernhardt is the President and CEO of Bernhardt Wealth Management, a registered investment adviser with the Securities and Exchange Commission. Registration is mandatory for all persons meeting the definition of investment adviser and does not imply a certain level of skill or training. The business leaders may or may not be clients of Bernhardt Wealth Management. These interviews are independent of investment advisory services and do not imply any endorsement of Gordon Bernhardt or Bernhardt Wealth Management by the business leaders.

This book exists because of all the inspirational individuals who so graciously shared their stories with me. I am thankful for the opportunity to get to know each and every one of you. I feel like a better person thanks to what I learned from you and your story.

To my team at Bernhardt Wealth Management—Tim Koehl, Bonnie Armstrong, Cindy Toukan, Emily Burns, and Jamie Bennett. I would never have been able to do this without your efforts and support throughout the process. Thank you for all you do for each other and for our clients.

I am deeply grateful to Herb Cohen, Founder and Host of Executive Leaders Radio, and to Peter Schwartz, Master Chair of Vistage Worldwide, for your help and encouragement on this project. Thank you.

And lastly, this book would not have been possible without the guidance and creative support of Karen Embry.

Table of Contents

Foreword

With a passion for educating his community's future business leaders, Gordon Bernhardt continues to share the stories and wisdom of successful corporate executives.

As the Founder and a Host of Executive Leaders Radio, I first had the privilege of getting to know Gordon when I interviewed him for my show in 2009. Gordon, the Founder and President of Bernhardt Wealth Management in McLean, Virginia, told me about returning to his Nebraska home-town in order to visit his former elementary-school teacher who was turning 90 years old. That story said a lot to me regarding Gordon's commitment to the human soul and to the human spirit. Gordon's a bonder who really cares about people and their well-being. I knew then that he embodies the same values as Executive Leaders Radio and would be an excellent partner in our endeavor to share the story-behind-the-story of other thriving executives.

While our show features interviews with some of the most successful business leaders in the country—sharing how they were able to build their enterprise, their management style, industry trends, challenges and opportunities ahead—we have discovered that the public really wants to get to know the person behind the mask. How old were they when they had their first job? What was their first car? What did they learn from mom that helped them in their business career? Who were their mentors? That's where Gordon steps in. He follows-up with our guests after their radio interview and digs a little deeper to unveil the secrets to their very personal success.

Gordon is on the cutting edge of what I call "reality print." Our world has been swept up in the reality-TV craze because of an obsession with observing the way real people live their lives—inspirational or flawed. Gordon's profiles address that fascination with the human condition by summarizing certain defining moments of some of the most efficacious executives. Nuggets of insight from individuals worth emulating will captivate readers and help us solve our own professional challenges. By learning from other peoples' mistakes or second-guessing their decisions, we can discover a lot about ourselves.

This is our goal when distributing the radio interviews and their corresponding case studies to students at various universities and then facilitating classroom visits or mentoring opportunities. Who better to learn from than the people who are doing it and succeeding at it? Future business men and women have the opportunity to study real-life examples of what can go wrong and how an executive's response to a problem either worked or didn't work. They discover every-day experiences that impacted who that individual became and how they operate in the business world, now.

With his own keen interest in learning about and from these outstanding individuals, I am impressed by the depth and the quality of Gordon's profiles and the substantial care he takes to get the stories right. Whether you are a student, a business professional, or simply someone who appreciates the lessons others have to teach, you will be heartened by this collection of *Profiles in Success*. Enjoy!

– **Herbert J. Cohen**
StartUp CEO
Founder and Host
Executive Leaders Radio
www.executiveleadersradio.com

As Executive Producer and Host of Executive Leaders Radio, Herb Cohen has been nicknamed the "Win-Win Connector" because in meeting over 900 CEOs each year (running $10million—$16billion businesses) he seeks to introduce mutually beneficial opportunities among C-level executives and students and young business professionals. An active entrepreneur in his own right since the age of 19, Cohen has co-founded several small-businesses and organizations including, QuiqMeds, Pennsylvania Private Investors Group, The Pros Video and The Pros Entertainers. His academic innovations consist of co-founding the University of Pennsylvania's Wharton Entrepreneurial Network, Fairleigh Dickinson Entrepreneurial Center, and the Center for the Advancement of Study of Entrepreneurship at Temple University. Not done yet, Cohen continues to focus on his next "equity" build."

Introduction

Free up your time for what matters most to you

Corporate executives are extremely busy people. Schedules are full, travel is frequent and stress is abundant. While diligent in overseeing the affairs of our companies, time constraints often restrict the same level of attentiveness when looking after our own personal situation. Having worked extensively with successful business leaders and entrepreneurs over that past 25 years, I find this problem to be extremely concerning.

As a wealth manager, and a business-owner, I know the countless decisions to be made regarding personal wealth management. Executive compensation packages can be complicated and often changing regulations lead to even more creative methods of recompense—only to require even much more extensive due diligence. Should you participate in a non-qualified deferral plan? Which insurance coverage will have any bearing on your long-term financial plan? What should you be doing now to help lower your future tax obligations? What additional investment options will supplement your investments within your company plans? What are you doing to plan for the single, most critically important financial event of your life—the transition out of your business?

Unfortunately, when executives lack the time to properly manage personal finances too frequently their decisions are motivated by taxes or emotions (theirs or their spouse's). Their portfolios are often designed and implemented in an ad hoc manner, without a clearly defined strategy—making it difficult if not impossible to achieve the goals that matter most.

Financial planning isn't just about making money. It's about your dreams and having the resources to implement those dreams. It's about devising a strategy that allows you to slow down or perhaps redirect your energy towards the people and the activities that bring you the most joy. It's about finding peace of mind.

Much like the corporate leaders featured in this volume of profiles, many of my clients are very involved in their communities. Not only do they provide financial support, they personally get involved with and work to further the missions of the organizations to which they contribute. They sit on advisory boards, chair fundraisers, or mentor someone in need of a positive role model. They look around, then roll up their sleeves and just do what needs to be done—and it is often a major long-term goal that they continue their charitable giving into their retirement.

Sharing that same kind of enthusiasm for community and service, I find it particularly satisfying to work with like-minded individuals and families who are passionate about doing what they know is right for others. Upon reflection, I would have to say that my drive to work in the financial services industry stems from my focus on community values and on giving something back on an intimate and everyday level. I'm fortunate that in my career, I'm able to find a way to help people in a one-on-one situation and it allows me to align my own values with how I want to lead my professional career. Even in a job you love, the opportunity to line up your skills with your personal passions doesn't come along every day. But when it does, it makes for exciting, fulfilling work. I experience that satisfaction at Bernhardt Wealth Management, as well as through my involvement with Executive Leaders Radio where I can help the next generation of corporate leaders through numerous educational mentoring opportunities.

What gives you real gratification?

Partnering with a professional advisor who knows your unique circumstances and understands your goals will help free up your time for what matters most to you. You gain peace of mind knowing a trusted partner is assisting with the ongoing review of your stock options and alternative investment purchases; continually reviewing market trends on your behalf; and working closely with your accountant and other advisors to ensure the best financial decisions are being implemented.

Ask yourself these questions:

- Have you been paying the proper amount of attention to your personal finances?
- Do you have someone you can turn to that will review your entire financial situation including investments, insurance, estate planning, tax mitigation and charitable giving, to help ensure you are making smart choices right now?
- Have you structured the right plan for turbulent markets?
- Does your current advisor invest the time to understand you, your family and your unique situation?
- Have you given any thought to how you're going to transition out of your company?

If you are not confident in the answers to these questions, then you might benefit from a professional second opinion. Understanding the particular needs of high-net-worth individuals, Bernhardt Wealth Management has developed a specialty practice working with executives in the Washington, D.C. area. We are committed to developing long-term client relationships built on a foundation of ethics, service and trust. We dedicate ourselves to focusing on our clients' investment goals so they can focus on creating a quality of life that reflects their deepest values.

Success gives us resources to implement dreams and serve the world around us. Wealth management is a critical component to unlocking the power of those resources.

– **Gordon J. Bernhardt, CPA, PFS, CFP®, AIF®**
Founder, President and CEO
Bernhardt Wealth Management, Inc.
www.BernhardtWealth.com

Since establishing his firm in 1994, Gordon Bernhardt has been focused on providing high-quality service and independent financial advice in order to help his clients make smart decisions about their money. He specializes in addressing the unique needs of successful professionals, entrepreneurs and retirees, as well as women in transition throughout the Washington, DC area. Over the years, Gordon has been sought out by numerous media outlets including MSN Money, CNN Money, Kiplinger and The New York Times for his insight into subjects related to personal finance.

Profiles

Neil Albert

Harnessing Your Niche

When you look back at your greatest decision, what do you hope it will be?

Will it be catching the wave of your most passionate calling in life and riding it all the way onto the shore?

Will it be finding that perfect person with whom you will spend the rest of your life with after waiting patiently as other people came and went?

Will it be assisting a company to almost quadruple in size with your own hands, expanding from $30 million to $110 million in revenue in only six years?

Now the President and CEO of MCR, LLC, Neil Albert can safely check "yes" after each of these accomplishments, a prime demonstration of how harnessing ones niche can yield a remarkable track record.

MCR was founded in 1977 by Dr. Gerald McNichols, who was also one of the founding members of the Office of the Secretary of Defense Cost Analysis Improvement Group (CAIG). CAIG performed independent cost estimating services for the Department of Defense (DoD), but Mr. McNichols felt the entrepreneurial blood flowing through his veins and decided to try his hand at building his own company. With that, MCR was launched in his home. By the mid 1980s, it had expanded significantly, handling an array of projects for the Write-Patterson Air Force Base and for the Navy.

Aiming to attract the best and brightest to his team, Dr. McNichols catalogued his network of associations throughout the cost analysis arena, and his sights fell on Neil almost immediately. When he decided to pursue a bid to open an office in Boston, he knew Neil was the man for the job.

"At the time, I was working at Textron Defense Systems in Wilmington, Massachusetts, supporting peacekeeper missile and other tactile weapons development as the head of their cost estimating organization," Neil remembers. "I loved what I was doing and wasn't interested in leaving." Dr. McNichols, however, expressed such conviction through his persistent offer that Neil agreed to submit his name with the proposal, believing there was no chance the project would receive funding.

As he had forecasted, two companies who had been loved for years and had already won the grant in the past did indeed win the two awards he had applied for. Much to his surprise, however, the committee announced the creation of a third award and bestowed it upon MCR's Boston initiative. "I had given my word, so I had to follow through," says Neil. "It seemed like a sacrifice at the time, but it turned out to actually be very fortuitous and a better plan overall."

Thus, Neil set to work opening the MCR office in Bedford, Massachusetts, just outside of Boston. For the first several months, he was a one-man show, helping the Hanscom Air Force Base with cost analysis work. By 1993, the solo practitioner had expanded into a thirty-person enterprise, and Mr. McNichols had put Neil in charge of the Washington, D.C. area as well. Commandeering both offices, Neil found that they were synergistic in resources and expertise which, when properly integrated, lent him an ideal platform upon which to grow the company. After he won an additional two major contracts and was able to build a more expansive workforce, he took on more responsibility at other office locations as well. When MCR was then reorganized into three partitions, he led the Eastern region, which was the size of the Central and Western regions combined.

After its steady climb, the company was doing approximately $27 million in business when Dr. McNichols received an offer he couldn't refuse and sold the company in 1999. MCR was purchased by GRC International, which automatically ushered Neil into the role of Senior Vice President of GRCI. GRCI was then bought by AT&T, and he suddenly found himself Senior Vice President of AT&T. "I inadvertently built up quite a resume," Neil laughs now.

This resume found its finishing touch when Dr. McNichols announced his departure from the company and chose Neil as his successor. Neil attributes this decision not only to the eleven years of intensive experience he had acquired serving the company, but also to his perpetual willingness to push the envelope. "I think Dr. McNichols chose me because I was a challenge to him," Neil reports. "I was always bucking the system, unafraid to disagree with him if I felt it was necessary. He saw that I was successful in doing this, and he thought I could bring the right kind of talent and leadership to MCR. He also liked that I could build a good team around me, and these are the things I strive to do here today."

Though many believed that MCR would lose its identity once it was acquired by AT&T, Neil and his team managed to hold their own, with MCR remaining intact as a wholly-owned subsidiary that they were finally able to buy out five years later. The company had remained relatively stagnant during that period, hovering around 250 employees.

Since it regained its independence, however, it has launched into a steep growth curve that would suggest MCR has more than made up for lost time. Now at 800 employees, Neil reflects on the adaptation inherently demanded by such a journey. "The company gets a little different the larger we get," he says. "It has been a challenge to me as it grows, but I welcome that challenge and have taken it on as we've continued to be successful."

Indeed, welcoming a challenge is nothing new to Neil. He started doing so at a young age, growing up in Sioux City, Iowa. "I loved my hometown, but my high school class would have had over 700 students, so I looked into attending private school for those last four years," he recalls. After researching schools on his own and collecting recommendations from friends and teachers, he decided upon Fountain Valley School, a private boarding school in Colorado. The atmosphere provided the ideal blend of challenge and support for success, and Neil left with ambitions of becoming a lawyer after a truly enriching and rewarding experience.

When he then began his freshman year of college at George Washington University (GWU), he quizzed his classmates on their intended career paths and found that everyone was pursuing a prelaw course of study. Not one to wander the beaten path, he decided to get a business degree instead, which was a risky and innovative move at the time given the newness of that academic branch. "I graduated with a degree in finance and returned to Colorado to make my fame and fortune, but unfortunately in 1975, the unemployment rate there was around 12 percent," he explains. "After a summer of job seeking to no avail, I returned to GWU and earned a graduate degree in financial management with a minor in economics."

Striking out to again seek his fame and fortune, Neil was recruited to work for a company that promised to train him toward attaining a Certified Financial Planner credential. In reality, however, they only trained him to be an insurance salesman, which fell completely outside the scope of his life goals. "Still, I always try to make the best out of any situation, so I took those six months I had there and tried to do the best I could," Neil says. They parted ways soon after.

That's when Computer Sciences Corporation (CSC) extended him an offer to become a management analyst to assist with work for the Department of Defense (DoD). While he supported the DoD in this capacity with their various divisions, their financials, and their budget activities, Neil met someone at CSC who was developing the ability to use Earned Value Management, a newly devised measure of performance of a program. He built proficiency in this area as well, utilizing his expertise to help produce several written pieces on performance measurements and a handbook before leaving the company to do some work for the Corps of Engineers.

Neil then got a call from a friend in Boston asking him if he'd come work for him as a cost estimator, which Neil eagerly accepted. In this role, he met Dr. McNichols, and the rest is history. "You don't go to school wanting to become a cost analyst, but cost estimating is hugely important," he points out, his true affinity for the field shining through. "Everybody needs to know the cost of building, producing, and delivering, whether you're building toasters or missiles. It is truly both an art and a science."

Now among the leading experts in the world on Work Breakdown Structure, a system for dissecting work into individual units to determine how much is needed to do a particular job, Neil has become somewhat of a pillar in his industry. If his legacy isn't for his honed expertise in this particular system, then it will surely be for his influence over MCR. "It's in the fact that I've grown something from the beginning to where it is today," he remarks. "It's like the life of the company has followed a path, and each step of the path has led me to improve, move up, or accomplish more. I can't imagine myself retiring because it's as if I have this inner drive that keeps pushing me forward, inspiring me to do better."

In advising young entrepreneurs entering the workforce today, Neil stresses the importance of volunteering. Whether it's in a community service environment, a classroom setting, or on the job, volunteering engenders a symbiotic relationship that benefits everyone involved. "I've learned so much about business from volunteering because doing so has allowed me to meet people, to gain new knowledge, and to learn life in a whole different environment," he explains. "Volunteer your skills, your resources, and your gifts. Whether it's community service or at work helping out on a project, you'll feel better and be rewarded."

Beyond this advise, Neil's journey itself is a testament to the power of passion plus niche. "What really drives me is how much I care about what I do and who I do it for," he concedes. "It's all about contribution and trying to help society become better, and once I find something I'm passionate about, I want to keep moving forward. I don't like to disappoint myself."

Neil's true inner connection with his industry is undeniable and is reflected not only in his success itself, but also in various forms of recognition, including his winning of the Society of Cost Estimating and Analysis's Lifetime Achievement Award in 2003 and the International Society of Parametric Analysts' lifetime recognition award, the Freiman Award, in 2010. Once one has discovered their niche, allowing this interest and proficiency to flourish can take you to new depths and breadths of mastery that are both highly rewarding and highly rewarded.

Edward John Allera

A Fresh Dose of Old-Fashioned Values

"When I was young, I always thought lawyers sat around in libraries, reading and smoking pipes," laughs Edward John Allera. Now the Co-Managing partner of the D.C. and San Diego offices of Buchanan Ingersoll & Rooney, he himself is living proof that this popular mental caricature couldn't be further from the truth. "Success is a 24/7 business," he emphasizes. "It's all about going out there and meeting people, learning all you can and listening to see how you might build partnerships with clients and associates that prove tremendously valuable to all parties involved." Having worked in a steel mill and an antifreeze canning plant in his youth and learning from the example of his parents' hard unwavering work ethic, Ed reminds us that when one genuinely enjoys one's profession, this kind of 24/7 work can feel less like labor and more like fun.

Buchanan Ingersoll & Rooney is a general service law firm of over 400 attorneys and government relations professionals serving primarily the East Coast, save for the San Diego location that Ed oversees. Initiated in Pittsburgh in the mid 1800's, it has since opened offices in New York, Philadelphia, Princeton, Harrisburg, Tampa, Miami, San Diego, and Washington, D.C., where Ed currently resides. Though the D.C. office originated as a tax boutique, its breadth has expanded concurrently with a strong level of expertise in FDA healthcare, government affairs, contracts, and corporate capability. The firm has 75 patent lawyers in its Alexandria office as well. These efforts supplement the firm's nationwide presence, which is focused more on conventional issues like litigation.

The son of a steel worker and a fulltime mother who truly embodied hard work and ethical living, Ed grew up in a family of modest means in a small town in Western Pennsylvania. After a few brief stints passing out papers as a boy, Ed's lasting professional journey commenced at age 15, when he first secured a job working in a pharmacy. He held this position throughout high school and then entered a five-year pharmacy program at West Virginia University. Upon graduating, he was awarded a prestigious internship at the United States Public Health Service in a Native American hospital in Western New Mexico, where he spent two years immersed in a climate of invaluable post-graduate learning.

With the Vietnam War propelling many of the nation's top minds into academia, he found himself under the tutelage of elite physicians who truly inspired him to think outside of the box. It was through this exposure that he first began theorizing about the impending role the federal government would play in healthcare, determining that law school would be a prudent next step for his future career path. "Becoming a small town pharmacist would have been rewarding in itself, but I felt there was something else out there for me," he explains.

While working through Georgetown Law School, Ed recalls one particularly remarkable professor who noted his uniquely blended background of science and law and advised him in pursuing a career with the FDA. "I'm forever indebted to that professor for his guidance," Ed reflects now. Heeding this advice, he accepted a position as Associate Chief of Counsel with the FDA upon receiving his law degree and spent over four stimulating years in that capacity until he decided it was time to evolve further. A contemporary offered him a position as the first associate at his fledgling FDA law boutique, and the pair built up the practice before eventually joining what, at the time, was the largest bankruptcy firm in the area.

When that firm suddenly went under in 1987, Ed saw it as a tremendous learning experience that came at a time when he could still afford to make big mistakes. "That was the only decision I ever made in my life solely for money," he reflects now. "You simply can't do that. You have to look at the platform, at where you want to go, and with whom you want to build your team. I learned that if you're making the decision for money, it's the wrong decision."

After freeing themselves from the wreckage, Ed and his group decided to seek haven on the other end of the spectrum and aimed to join the most conservative law firm they could find. They spent the following seven years in a very traditional Cleveland-based firm until Ed began considering a transition to something with a different culture and a broad national reach. "Buchanan Ingersoll & Rooney had a very Midwestern company culture, and I'm a very Midwestern kind of guy," Ed says. After joining the firm, its Washington office went from 25 to 60 attorneys, and his book of business expanded accordingly. "Finding the right platform is the most important thing," he explains. "Then it becomes finding the right people to form the right team to work on that platform. You're always stronger as part of a team," he emphasizes. "Every lawyer's going to have one or two bad years, but with a diverse group, you have a self-vetted balance; an internal continuity plan."

With this formula for success leveraged firmly throughout his approach, Ed became managing partner in 2004 after cultivating the most extensive book of business in the office. Also responsible for running the FDA practice and drawing new business, he now spends his days meeting with associates and colleagues with a focus on follow-up, delegation, and business development. Despite the constant influx of new information to read and absorb, Ed's passion for healthcare and FDA law never falters, which give him the inexhaustible passion for the industry that lends his expertise such potency. "I have always been blessed with good and abundant energy," he remarks. "My innate interest in the subject matter of my work only exacerbates this vigor."

This innate interest expresses itself not only in a rare depth of familiarity with his craft, but also in a rare gift at attracting new clients and furthering the firm's development initiatives. "Lawyers always talk too much and listen too little," he remarks. With this philosophy in mind, he focuses on the importance of hearing what others have to say. This openness fosters a sense of collaboration and affords Ed the insight he needs to acutely and effectively assess the needs of a potential client or business partner and gauge how Buchanan Ingersoll & Rooney might address those needs. "Business development for attorneys is a learned skill," he emphasizes. "You have to go out and talk to people and show them your value."

The importance of listening manifests itself not only in Ed's attitude toward business development, but also in his management philosophy and leadership style. "I've certainly made mistakes along the way, but a friend and mentor who teaches leadership at West Point really drove home the importance of leadership in four directions," he explains. "In order to accomplish this, you must always be cognizant and listen to the people above you, the people below you, your peers, and yourself." Practicing this kind of leadership has allowed Ed to build the kind of team he had hoped to build, developing quality people with enduring integrity and fidelity.

Through the art of listening, one is truly able to grasp what is expected of them—a skill that Ed defines as among the most important that young entrepreneurs can have and cultivate as they enter the workforce today. "Know what is expected of you," he urges. "Every law firm and every employer has a requirement. Know what these goals are and meet them." He also expresses the paramount importance of building a comprehensive and deeply entrenched knowledge base of one's industry. "Once you've picked your specialty, learn it. Devour everything. Find out what the industry leaders are reading and read the same thing," he adds.

With so many accomplishments already secured, what comes next for Edward John Allera as he continues fashioning his own unique imprint on the face of healthcare law? "I'd like to see the firm grow in any administrative practice in Washington," he remarks. As the current climate finds many Washington firms linking with corporate New York firms to cement and drive deal orientation, competition in the industry is at an all-time high. "Washington was built on the Federal government, so we'll continue our focus of administrative law, government contracts, and government affairs, with an emphasis on building up our administrative law practice," he describes. Conversely, he envisions the addition of more corporate and litigation capability for the firm's San Diego branch.

With a wonderful family and a solid core from which to work, Ed's future also promises the furthering of a personal legacy that promotes the enduring values that have led him to where he is today. "I feel that what I will ultimately be most proud of in my life is still around the corner," he remarks. "I worry about the future of law firms as they continue to trend towards quantity over quality. They're losing the emphasis on collegiality that I find so important, and I hope to promote this collegiality through my own practice."

In a word, one can classify Ed as old-fashioned, but he wields this quality to restore a human element to the industry and the kind of resolute work ethic that is so sorely lacking in today's professional environment. Ever a straight arrow as he works to further the intersection of science and law, his example reminds us that timeless concepts like true listening, solid integrity, and the fostering of strong working relationships are just as important in today's business environment as they were in the past, bringing lasting success to those with the wisdom to put them into practice.

Karen Barbour

Turning Adversity into Success

From a very young age, Karen Barbour learned the importance of determination and hard work, which she now puts into practice everyday as the President of The Barbour Group, a Maryland-based surety bond agency. Formed in 2002, The Barbour Group has amassed roughly $4 million in revenue each year, for the past three years, and has over two hundred clients.

But her path to The Barbour Group was a winding one filled with experiences that helped to shape Barbour's intrinsic desire to advocate for those without a voice and to represent the under-represented.

Born in Baltimore, Maryland in the 1960's, Barbour recalls being very shy and always staying close to her mother.

"I think if I could have hugged my mother's leg every place that we went, I would have been glued to her, and that would have been fine with me," Barbour recalls.

Barbour also remembers not doing well early on in school and having a very difficult time with her teachers and classmates. Being taller than the other children and not fitting in, she would often be misunderstood by the teachers and sent home with reprimands.

"It wasn't that I wasn't smart, I just hated school, and didn't see the point," she explains, "…there weren't a lot of options being presented to young girls for their futures at that time. I remember being asked what I wanted to be when I grew up, 'a secretary? a nurse?,' while my brothers were being asked if they wanted to become doctors or lawyers. I wanted to be the President of the United States and back then I didn't see the point of doing well in school if all I could be was a secretary or a mom."

Barbour recalls special trips with her mother where they would go to the library to get books about powerful women in history. Madam Curie was a specific favorite of theirs as she shared their Polish heritage.

"I think my mom was teaching me gender history before it was even around, and it really impacted me."

When Barbour was eleven years old, she was playing in the backyard when she heard a loud noise from the front of the house. That noise was her mother being hit by a car and Barbour's life would never be the same. While undergoing major surgeries to rectify the damage of the car accident, doctors discovered that Barbour's mother was in the advance stages of cancer, and she died shortly thereafter.

After her mother's death, Barbour's father fell into a deep depression and within a year, her older brother passed away as well at the age of 16.

"My father was a World War II veteran, but I think he experienced more tragedy at home than at Normandy."

With her mother, close aunt, and brother all dying in rapid succession, and her oldest brother away at college, Barbour found herself in the position of having to take care of her father, the household responsibilities, and also help out in the family grocery store, at the young age of twelve.

"It was hard, but it made me feel good to see that I had done something productive," Barbour describes, "after my mom passed, I didn't feel right being still in the house. If I wasn't working, it wasn't okay. Also, I think I had the fighter mentality of my grandmothers' who emigrated from Poland as third class citizens. I guess I have that 'gene' that helps you live through anything. After the loss of her beloved mother, Barbour had a change of heart at school and she exerted herself and became a very dedicated student.

"I thought to myself, 'Enough is enough. I've been playing this game too long."

With her change in performance, Barbour was moved to the advance groups in her classes and was accepted into a private high school where she went on to get (mostly) A's and to graduate with honors.

During her time in college Barbour continued to take care of her father and the household, while working part-time in the family grocery store, working part-time at another job, and traveling to classes five miles each way on a bicycle.

Barbour's intention to attend law school after graduation was put on hold as she was wait-listed for admittance at University of Baltimore. While waiting to hear back from the university and substitute teaching to support herself, Barbour heard from a friend who offered her a ticket that he could no longer use to travel to Africa. Barbour accepted the offer and while traveling in Africa, felt a huge weight fall off of her shoulders.

"When I was in Africa, the stress poured off of me and for the first time I felt stress-free."

Barbour promptly called the University of Baltimore and withdrew her application. While in Africa, Barbour met the man that would become her husband and together they returned to the US.

Barbour's path to surety bond management began while working as an Underwriter at a large insurance company. While at this company she learned the inner workings of the insurance business, the finance and accounting of risk analysis, and how to work with the contractor clients.

"I was looking at accounts that were being built all over the country and I loved it! You got to know the clients, all about their history of past performance, their credit and financials, and so you could make decisions about what you felt they were capable of, in order to get them to the next level."

It was while working at this company that Barbour also learned how powerful and impactful surety bonding can be.

"I remember one day walking home from work and seeing a demonstration in front of The Belvedere Hotel. The demonstration was about the Minority Business Enterprise (MBE) goals being increased to include women as minorities. I stopped to listen because I wanted to hear the response from the Black population in attendance. Their major concern was that the White women would be a front for their White husbands in order to circumvent the rules and receive MBE benefits. I could definitely see that the Blacks were fighting hard enough for the 'meat' that they got, and thought that it would be great if there was some kind of program to help minorities—from a bonding standpoint. When I went to work the next day, everyone was discussing the rally because some of the surety's general contractor clients were not happy about the MBE goals getting increased. I'll never forget the response… they said, 'Well, we're going to have to just advise our clients to bond the minorities, but they won't be able to bond, so then our clients can get a waiver.' I thought to myself 'so much for the civil rights movement, what about the opportunity movement?' It was then that I realized that I could not help empower anyone within that organization and so I left." Barbour went to work for another company that was dedicated to working with small businesses, but she never forgot what happened after that rally.

"I thought that if they could paint a brush like that and wipe out people's lively-hood or their chance of succeeding, then this bonding industry is very powerful, extremely powerful, and it can be a barrier for many people."

After working for eleven years as an Underwriter, Barbour became a Bond Producer, recalling that on her first day she was handed the Yellow Pages and told to make at least ten calls per day.

"I thought I would be introduced to the agency's clients so that I could build up a referral base," Barbour recalls. Instead, she became known as the "bond girl" and had to contend with initially being given contracts that were impossible to underwrite.

"I got out of the 'bond girl' mentality really quickly and I did that by focusing all on production. I was hardly in the office and I just produced. I was putting on nine new accounts each month and that forced the other producers to have to recognize that I was one of them."

After fighting to be recognized as an equal and rising to become one of her company's top producers, Barbour soon realized that ownership opportunities were slim at her agency. She decided to transition to another agency where those opportunities would be more readily available, or so she thought.

"I had been working there for several years and I remember asking when I might be considered for ownership or what path I needed to follow in order to achieve that, but I never got a response."

After two of her male colleagues received promotions to ownership status, she reached out to the agency to find out about the benchmarks for ownership one last time. When she arrived at the meeting, instead of discussing the benchmarks, Barbour was blindsided by unfounded accusations about her lack of people-skills.

Barbour recounts, "I was forty years old with two small daughters, a failing marriage, and I was giving over 100% to this company. I thought, 'You know what, I don't need this', and I left the company to start my own agency."

Though Barbour made the decision to branch out on her own after this incident, she began considering the choice when her goals to make a legislative impact on the direction and future of small business and small business owners became limited by her employer's desires and goals.

"I participate in several trade organizations and would attend many industry conferences and meetings. I kept noticing the representative for the Army Corps of Engineers trying to reach out to contractors and find out what they wanted from the Army. He wasn't having much success and I asked him if he ever thought of having the contractors gather in one location with the Army in order to open up the dialogue. I said, 'I have an idea, let's form a coalition and call it the General Counsel for Construction with the Army Corps of Engineers' and he loved the idea and implemented it immediately."

This was a huge achievement for Barbour and she served as the liaison to the coalition for two years, making significant impacts in the way contractors submit bids to the Army and enabling small contractors to be more effective with their bidding. But Barbour came under attack for her participation in the coalition and even had her employment threatened due to her involvement.

This was a turning point in Barbour's career. She realized that her aspirations to influence policy would be difficult, if not impossible, to fulfill while working for someone other than herself.

"I thought to myself, 'I don't see myself as doing less of this in my life, I see myself as doing more of this in my life and I need to be in a position where people can't call up my boss and threaten my employment.'"

When Barbour started her own agency, many of her existing clients gladly came over with her.

"I brought with me about sixty to sixty-five of my clients, as well as, ten corporate surety markets. I had a plan and I was ready to hit the ground running."

Unfortunately, the timing of the start of Barbour's company coincided with the down-turn in government contracts as most federal monies were being re-directed into Homeland Security after the events of 9/11.

"It was a down year," Barbour explains, "but I have always made a profit since I have been in business."

Once formed, The Barbour Group quickly dedicated themselves to small and mid-sized businesses so that Barbour could spend more time being politically active. "I wanted to show my clients that 'I'll give you the bid, performance and payment bonds that you need to grow your company, but I'm going to put strategies in place to help small business, from a legislative stand-point, to not only help your playing field but to show that I truly care about my industry and what I am doing.'"

In 2006, Barbour was instrumental in the writing and passing of a Maryland Bill allowing private individuals to provide surety bonds to small business contractors, if they couldn't get a corporate bond. Though the passing of this bill was a great success for small business contractors, its implementation was stalled and then essentially negated by the lack of support from various state agencies. Even after emergency regulations were passed in 2007, for the first time in 12 years, by the then Governor Martin O'Malley, it was years later that the new regulations were found in bid solicitations. After this disappointing start, Barbour decided to step back from much of her legislative activities to focus on her own business development and has recently brought in a public relations firm to help market her agency, as well as a lobbyist.

Barbour is scaling up and forming relationships with national firms to help build her brand, "I was recently awarded the Ernst & Young Entrepreneurial Winning Women Award and was appointed by the Governor as Co-Chair of his Commission on Small Business."

In addition to the many other trade associations that Barbour participates in, she is also a strong contributor to the Muscular Dystrophy Association and has taken part in many "Lock Up" events and has co-hosted a "Party for the Cure" each year, for the past three years, raising steadily increasing donation amounts with a total of over one hundred thousand dollars raised.

Barbour attributes her success to the on-going support of her family and key mentors who have given her guidance and encouraged her to step out on her own, but most of all she speaks of her mother.

"My mom was a wonderful mother and that empowers me still." Barbour says, "We have such a limited time on this earth and we're going to be dead forever. I just want to go for it. I didn't wake up until I was forty-three years old and I wish I could have had sprung to life at the age of thirty-three, but I am building momentum quickly..."

Barbour's message to those who are just graduating and ready to step out into the world:

"If you want to be an entrepreneur—do it now. Don't get sucked up by some corporate structure that you can't find your way out of until your forty. If you feel the least twinge of being an entrepreneur, you should do it. Adversity can really give you discipline and discipline can give you empowerment. You can be anything you want to be, so use the adversity to make something good happen. Don't get stuck there, apply yourself and work hard, work hard, work hard. And always look for that open door because an open door will always lead to another door. Don't just stand there, thinking about what may be on the other side and be apprehensive about it and what's behind those doors; if you do that you won't get anywhere in life. You don't have to be afraid."

Barbour has certainly lead a life that has seen more than its fair share of adversity, but instead of letting it hold her back, she has turned that adversity into her own motivation to succeed. That success has not only influenced Barbour and her company, but it has made monumental changes in the lives of each of the small business contractors that Barbour has stood up for, spoken out to protect, and ensured that those with the power to "paint away lively-hoods" are working to help and not hurt.

Karen Barbour, a powerful woman in history, a powerful woman who's made history.

Bill Barton

The Business Benefits of Life Balance

Since the recent economic downturn first began its desecration the American job market, the traditional recipe for success has undergone an ambiguous transformation. Bigger is now sometimes synonymous with better, and young entrepreneurs entering an ultra-competitive global marketplace are often led to believe that working 24/7 is the only way to stay ahead. Even the field of law, so competitive even in a healthy economy, hasn't been immune to these rising stakes, and most young lawyers enter the field today with the understanding that they'll need to check their personal lives at the door. Bill Barton, however, resolved to blaze a different kind of trail when he founded Barton Baker Thomas & Tolle LLP. His success—unique in that it spans both the professional and personal spheres—shows that, especially in today's market, it pays to live a balanced life.

Bill's father, a prominent labor lawyer in the DC metro area, served as general counsel to the US Chamber of Commerce and retired at age 65 to open his own law firm, where he practiced for the following three decades. His excellent passion, diligence, and commitment were an example to Bill throughout his formative years. Due in part to the effects of this role model and in part to his own inner aspirations, Bill himself was no stranger to hard work. "I was raised in a home with a very healthy respect for education, self-reliance, and strong work ethic," he recalls now. "Thus, summers were not for leisure, but for work or summer school."

In accordance with this principle, Bill spent several summers working in construction, as those were the main jobs that were available. "My summer jobs were educations in themselves and were a great way for me to realize what I didn't want to spend the rest of my life doing," he remarks. "When you earn your living by working long days in the sweltering heat, you begin to equate all your expenses with the number of hours out in the heat that it would take you to earn a given sum. Comparatively speaking, higher education definitely seemed like a better route to take."

Though he and his parents discussed private school options, Bill ultimately elected to remain in public school because he felt that it would expose him to a more diverse group of people. "I also felt that it was a place where you learned to negotiate your way through situations and conflicts," he continues, touching on a skill that has become invaluable to his profession as an attorney. Despite this hint of foresight, however, Bill didn't decide to go to law school until his junior year of college at Ohio Wesleyan University. "My father never put pressure on me to become a lawyer, but it was certainly advantageous to be able to observe the profession firsthand through him," Bill points out. "It gave me a clear snapshot of what I could expect, both good and bad."

Graduating from college in the midst of the Vietnam War era, he didn't have the luxury of taking the extra time to reflect on his career path that has become a common fixture in the path of today's youth. "A lot of us were under the gun with the draft, so you had to make these decisions pretty quickly," he remembers. "You had to get focused immediately, but I think that was a good thing. I don't regret the decision to go to law school at all."

Having undergone the Reserve Officer's Training Corps (ROTC) and deferred his four-year commitment so he could attend law school, Bill earned his JD from American University and then began his term of service on Air Force active duty as a Judge Advocate Generals Corps (JAG) officer, later staying on for an extra year of service after the term's completion. "It was a tremendous experience, and especially suited to me in that I wasn't ready to spend six days a week in an office billing two thousand plus hours right after law school," he says. His thirst for travel and worldly experience was satiated when he was sent to California and then to Thailand, where he had the opportunity to try a plethora of court-martial cases and travel throughout Asia. He then spent the last two and a half years of his service in Florida, where he cultivated a sweeping knowledge of Air Force Systems Command and government contract work. "They basically threw me in and said, 'Okay, you're our contracts guy,' and that started my career in government contracts," he laughs.

When Bill emerged from the Air Force, he returned to the DC metro area after realizing that he would need to live in a large city if he wanted to engage in the kind of sophisticated legal work he had set his sights on. He noticed that the Navy was doing most of its procurement work through civilians rather than through uniformed services, and a huge backlog of claims had built up during the ship building boom of the Reagan years. They were looking for experienced lawyers to help with the headache, and Bill signed on for three years in the Navy General Counsel's office, where he tried massive shipbuilding claims. This experience introduced him to the premiere government contract firms in the country against whom he litigated massive shipbuilding claims.

After being promoted to Deputy Associate General Counsel, he decided it was time to enter private practice and accepted a position with a firm specializing in government contracts and energy work. Several years later, he transitioned over to a large general practice firm that focused heavily on litigation, where he learned the ways of the big corporate firm. "All of those experiences furnished a great background for my next step, which was starting my own firm," says Bill. "If you're going to start your own business, you should know that business pretty well, and for service industries, it's especially helpful to have the contacts that only experience can produce. You should have some idea of where the work is going to come from and how you're going to put it together."

Armed with that knowledge and those contacts, Bill launched Barton Baker Thomas & Tolle with one other partner in 1984. Both had spent time working for large law firms, and both wanted something more out of life. "Our feeling was that there was a better way to practice law than the way that large firms were doing it, which tended toward the impersonal," Bill explains. The firm was launched with a niche focus of representing government contractors, and it remains true to that niche today. "We don't try to be all things to all people, but instead stay within the two core areas of government contracts practice and corporate transactional work, which encompasses maintenance, reorganization, and finance," he says. "Still, this corporate work is done primarily within the government contract community. Understanding the business and due diligence, we're a good fit for government contractors who want to either sell or buy a company."

Like most lawyers, the partners at Bill's firm are on call 24/7. They do most of their work personally because they feel it's the most effective and efficient way to deliver their services to clients, and because these clients rely on them, they are devoutly committed to producing the best value and service possible. Unlike most lawyers, however, these partners also value their private time, striving to strike a work-life balance that allows personal endeavors, family time, and hobbies to coexist with top-notch legal services.

Many big law firms would view this balanced perspective as uneconomical because it endorses activities that do not contribute directly to the business's bottom line, yet Bill understands that, especially in today's tough economy, being well-rounded is a pivotal component to any successful business model. "So much of what we do, especially in a services industry like law, is dealing with people," he emphasizes. "Candidates may be smart, but if you aren't a people person and can't relate well with others, you're at a major disadvantage."

With this in mind, Bill is a strong believer that bigger is not necessarily better. With five full-time professionals and two of counsel, his firm has never vacillated over eleven attorneys. "Maintaining a manageable-sized practice is at the heart of our core values, and it's what allows us to keep the intimate client relationships that make us so unique," he points out.

Placing a premium on work-life balance not only preserves valuable time to foster strong attorney-client relationships, but also allows these attorneys to cultivate strong and well-rounded interests that are then used to enforce these relationships further. "My clients understand and appreciate the fact that I'm not one-dimensional," Bill points out. "I like to travel, play tennis, play golf, and paint, among other things. One of our clients is a world-class fencer, while another is a ranked USTA player who participates in tournaments all over the country. We all have lives outside of law, and a lot of our clients share these same interests. We can relate to one another, building stronger and more genuine ties."

Bill readily admits that he could be making more money as a senior partner at a mega firm, but at what cost? "In addition to the gift of great relationships with clients, working at a firm like Barton Baker Thomas & Tolle also grants the gift of great relationships with family and friends," Bill explains. "I've been married to the same woman for over forty years, and we have a great relationship. I participated in my son's little league and was a big part of his life growing up. Sure, we all want comfortable lives, but it comes down to what you're willing to give up to enjoy life. I don't think anyone ever grows old and wishes they had spent more time in the office."

In advising young entrepreneurs entering the business world today, Bill emphasizes the importance of education and self-reliance, advocating for graduate school as a good way to further distinguish oneself. "Not everyone lands a dream job the first time around, but you can learn something from any situation," he says. "It's important to have a good attitude and to make the most out of every experience, and your superiors will notice and appreciate that."

Beyond this, he stresses the importance of swimming against the current of depersonalization that seems to be sweeping across all industries. "We try to distinguish ourselves by retaining that traditional culture of professionalism, devotion, and personal commitment, and people like that," says Bill. Pairing a studious work ethic with a studious life ethic in this manner yields a balance that is at once practical and profitable, ambitious and wise.

Brien Biondi

The Standing Ovation

The hall was filled with five hundred people; maybe more. As the audience rose to their feet in collective recognition, their applause filling the air with insistent jubilance, Brien Biondi couldn't believe his eyes. He was certainly no stranger to success. In fact, he had invested much of his professional career to the promotion and celebration of the achievements of others, especially through his work to support CEOs and company presidents through his leadership of the Entrepreneurs' Organization (EO). When those same CEOs and presidents were granting him a standing ovation for that work, Brien remembers today, a certain feeling of uncharacteristic timidity overcame him.

"I'm very comfortable on stage talking about everybody else, but I don't like it so much when it's about me," he explains today. "Every great leader has a great team, and for me, I like to recognize that team." Now the President and COO of League Asset Corp, Brien's advocacy for collective triumph is evident throughout his professional career, and nowhere is it accentuated more than in League's commitment to bringing real estate investment opportunities to the average investor.

League Assets Corp. may be only five years young, but it has already distinguished itself as an innovative, multi-platform vehicle through which individuals with investment portfolios of virtually any size can reap the benefits of the real estate industry. With both a publicly and privately traded REIT, the firm also boasts a syndication platform that identifies and secures new projects on a quarterly basis.

What truly puts League in a league of its own, however, is its utilization of the Internet to accomplish its goal of reaching the average investor. Through Google banner advertising, social media tools like Facebook, and the free gift of their sleek publication *The Blue Book of Real Estate Syndication*, the company generates over a thousand leads each month. Member service managers then reach out to these leads and educate them on their real estate investment opportunities. When an individual decides to invest in one of their platforms, that person then becomes a member partner with League.

"What's nice about this approach is that we're letting average individuals buy into a project, and we're not a blind pool," Brien points out. Through this model, his team has recruited 2,700 member partners to date, and the firm raises $5 to $10 million per month through their syndication platform alone. Every project is different, but the general timeframe is around three years, and League always has new investment opportunities launching as established projects wrap up and pay out. Teeming with activity and constantly reflexive, the cap for League is yet to be imagined. "We're currently looking to build out globally, and we're hiring a lot of talent," Brien reports.

While its growth margins are impressive, League's success is about much more than just numbers on paper. At its core, this achievement is rooted in a set of core values that promote integrity amongst its employees and trust amongst its investors. "Our credo is part of our culture, and we measure ourselves against it in our day-to-day operations and strategic decisions," says Brien. This mission statement pledges complete transparency, a commitment to treat others with dignity and respect, and the principle that the firm's word is its bond and must be worthy of trust. "This is how we operate as an organization and is very much from the heart," he affirms. "Our Internet presence really allows people to connect with this credo, and it is absolutely fundamental to the business we run and the relationships we develop."

Brien was raised in Connecticut right outside of Hartford. As the oldest of six children, he was also the most aggressive, expressing a strong leadership streak that would evolve to become a definitive aspect of his character later in life. "Our family always encouraged structure, and I grew up in an environment where everyone had jobs," Brien remembers. "I sold fruit, cut lawns, delivered newspapers—you name it. I didn't make straight A's like my sisters easily did, but I had a lot of EQ, or emotional quotient."

Nowhere was this EQ more emphasized than in Brien's junior high stint as a radio co-host for a Saturday morning show called Teen Talk. After obtaining his FCC broadcasting license, he would go out and interview a slew of fascinating personalities, ranging from the state governor to tennis stars like Arthur Ash. Initially averse to the idea of attending boarding school for high school, he quickly changed his mind once he saw that the campus had a radio station of its own. It was at this boarding school that Brien first learned to embrace independence, diversity, and leadership, building relationships with classmates from around the globe and graduating as President of the School. "It was one of the most impactful experiences of my life," he says now. "I left as a totally different individual, and I had big aspirations for college."

In his sophomore year at American University, Brien got a job running the sports program at a local elementary school, and his leadership skills affirmed themselves again when he decided to launch a nighttime baseball league there. The school lost its athletic funding the subsequent year, but Brien decided to take matters into his own hands by starting a 10-week after-school sports session, charging $50 per child. Overwhelmed with interest, Brien hired several American students to coach in the program, and he offered even more programs the next semester. The enterprise was so successful that his mother suspected he was selling drugs. "Ma, I'm telling you, I've got this business," he would tell her with a laugh.

Brien then graduated with a degree in accounting and spent the next several years working with KPMG, which he describes as a tremendous learning experience in that he was constantly being exposed to new businesses and how they operate. He then went to work as a controller for the Archdiocese of Washington for five years, during which he was able to observe the inner workings of the church. "I also had the opportunity to learn about the good that comes from doing your business in an ethical and just way, which factors largely into the credo that sets our business apart," says Brien. "It was a very insightful experience."

After that engagement, Brien accepted the position of CFO of World Presidents Organization, which marked his first real exposure to CEOs and global leadership coaching. "I began traveling and going to educational events, and I became acquainted with the challenges that CEOs were facing, as well as the importance of peer-to-peer learning," he points out. "I came to understand how truly lonely it is at the top, and how valuable it is for CEOs to be able to sit down at the table together regardless of their industry to talk about the issues they share in common."

Brien married his wife Amy in 1997, and that same year, he accepted a position as CEO of the Young Entrepreneurs Organization (YEO), which later fused with the World Entrepreneurs Organization to become EO. "The experience of running these organizations had a huge impact on my life, growth, and learning," Brien affirms, of his seven years leading the organization. When one takes into account the effect he, in turn, had on EO, one can safely assume that the feeling was mutual. During his tenure, Brien grew the organization's staff from five to almost 60, and membership increased dramatically from 1,200 to 6,000. They opened offices in Asia, Europe, Latin America, and Canada, and they distinguished themselves as the primary organization serving young entrepreneurs today. By assembling, educating, and supporting these young entrepreneurs, Brien and his team facilitated the creation of wealth and job opportunities worldwide.

After finishing his time with EO, he spent almost four years leading Chief Executive Organization (CEO), which promoted global educational collaboration between some of the world's most prominent CEOs and connected them with important business and political figures. His expertise was used to build the brand and to facilitate new events focused on economic, political, and social learning. Brien and his wife then took a year off to travel with their two young children—something he will always remember as a seminal experience in his life. "This time really allowed me to focus and consider what I wanted next in my career," he muses. "It was the first time in years that I could really free my mind, and it allowed me to thoroughly explore the opportunity with League before taking it."

As Brien got better acquainted with League, he was impressed with the sheer volume of opportunity that lay imbued in its business model. The company had been launched by two individuals—a genius-type 30-year-old who excelled in the real estate and finance aspects of the industry and a brilliant marketing personality who laid foundational building blocks for the company's credo. But they needed someone to run the company while they were out in the field. "Through our discussions, it seemed like a good fit strategy-wise, and I wanted to come into a company in its early stages so that I could facilitate and share in its growth," says Brien.

Since joining League, Brien's greatest contribution has been his extensively honed leadership experience, breaking down silos and promoting collaboration and structure. "I encourage pushback but I won't tolerate resistance," he says. "It is of the utmost importance that the team challenge me and each other as we discern the right decision for us, but at the end of the day, we know that there is trust. This is key—it's what allows us to gel and move forward as a team."

In advising young entrepreneurs entering the workforce today, Brien advocates for the same kind of aggressive drive toward one's goals that he exhibited as a child. "Unequivocally, I would urge you to go out and start a business," he affirms. "Don't worry about failure. You're young, and it only gets harder to take a risk like that as you get older." He does not, however, recommend that someone enter the business world blindly. Rather, finding a good mentor is the key to success. "It could be anybody," Brien says. "It could be the person running the store down the street. Just find someone who is older, more mature, with experience, and with success. Introduce yourself and ask them to mentor you, and meet with them on a monthly basis at a minimum to gauge your success and keep you accountable."

Beyond this, Brien echoes the importance of perseverance. "If a business survives through its first 12 months, odds are that it's going to go," he reveals. "Just keep persevering through that first year or two. Then, once you've established yourself, I believe in the mantra of 'learn, earn, live, give.' This should be a predominant part of your thinking and culture." By adhering to these principles and pursuing one's inner entrepreneurial spirit with innovation, integrity, and drive, today's young entrepreneurs can begin making their purposeful way toward tomorrow's standing ovations.

Joe Brown

Among Friends, About Success

Reflecting back on the carefree days of childhood, it is not unusual to have a special place in our hearts for the neighborhood kids we grew up with. What is unusual, however, is for such childhood friends to stay close into adulthood and launch a $30 million company together. With society's increasingly globalized and mobile lifestyle, it is far more normal to sweep from one place to another, making new acquaintances that often replace the old as we go. But for Joe Brown, now the President of Accelera Solutions, going into business with lifelong friends has proven to be an endeavor that is as fruitful as it is fun.

Joe grew up with Chong Yi, Steve Daly, and Terrill Andrews in a quiet neighborhood in Falls Church, Virginia. "We were a tight-knit group as kids, and we've been close all our lives," Joe remarks now. "We have a lot of trust in each other and no hidden agendas, which makes it really easy to work together."

They parted ways after high school, attending different colleges and then venturing out into the workforce. Joe and Steve followed parallel paths, both accepting positions at the same small consulting firm based out of Alexandria. The firm was then acquired by Sequoia Software, which in turn was acquired by a larger corporation called Citrix Systems, a firm specializing in the development of enterprise virtualization software.

Joe shot up the ranks at Citrix, yet he soon realized that the corporate environment of larger enterprises was not his style. He decided to leave the technology titan but couldn't shake his attention from the looming void he foresaw in the marketplace. One evening in 2002, he invited Chong, Steve, and Terrill to a meeting in his home in Burke, Virginia, and set out his proposal for Accelera Solutions. A week later, each man wrote a check for a thousand dollars and deposited it into a business bank account, marking the birth of the company. "It's been an interesting journey since then," says Joe with a smile.

Accelera started as a consulting firm focused solely in virtualization technology and solutions, providing the secure remote access, telework solutions, and application centralization or virtualization that allows people to access enterprise applications via small and inexpensive computers that have nothing actually loaded on them. These computers therefore require very little maintenance—what the industry terms *thin client technology.* Because it eliminates the need for maintenance, thin client technology dramatically reduces the total cost of ownership of IT infrastructure. "Armed with this concept, along with some intellectual property and knowledge we had developed through working in the space for other customers, we went out espousing the benefits of virtualization and looking for business," Joe reports.

If one could turn back the hands of time and ask those four young friends what the future would hold for them, none could have predicted the formation and subsequent flourishing of Accelera. "To a certain extent, the launching of the business was happenstance," Joe reports.

"We all happened to be in the same place at the same time, both geographically and in life." None of them were married or had any kids, and when the opportunity came along, they realized that it might be their only chance to take such a risk before family responsibilities began to pile on. The four young, single homeowners decided to give it a shot, trusting in Joe's vision and willing to take a leap of faith. "We're happy now that we did," Joe confirms.

As a consulting firm, Accelera spent its fledgling months focused solely on software implementation and support. When customers wanted to purchase the software product itself, Joe and his team would direct them toward other organizations like Citrix. Within a year and a half of opening its doors, however, more and more clients said they'd like to buy both the product and the service directly from Accelera. With that, the consulting firm signed up as a technology reseller with Citrix, and within three years, they had earned platinum partner status, distinguishing themselves among the manufacturer's most valuable resellers. Within four years, they had earned the title of North American Partner of the Year, and within five, they had already surpassed companies who had been in that line of work for over a decade.

Serving as a consulting firm as well as a reseller has not only allowed Accelera to provide a wider range of services to its customers, but has also been a major stepping stone in securing its position as a leader in virtualization technology in the D.C. metropolitan area. "Our goal was to have a really strong relationship with the manufacturer, but even if you're the greatest consulting firm in the world, manufacturers have very little time for you unless you're actually influencing or selling their technologies," Joe explains. "We realized that if we didn't post some numbers and do some good revenue for them, then we'd be just like all the other partners out there, and we just weren't satisfied with that. We wanted to be able to offer more to our customers."

Who exactly are these customers? 65 percent of Accelera's business is done in the Federal government space in support of both the

Department of Defense and civilian agencies. The remaining chunk lies primarily in the commercial enterprise, with a final five to seven percent falling in the public sector, including state and local governments.

Joe, Chong, Steve, and Terrill have always had a strong foundation of trust between them, and this trust seems to transmit seamlessly into their customer relationships as well. "We've always been really good at earning the trust of our customers and implementing solutions that really save people money and increase efficiencies," Joe observes. "It's what we hang our hats on. Even in poor economic times, people want to listen when you say you can save them money on IT, which is typically the biggest expense in any organization. So it makes sense, then, that our message resonates well with most folks."

Accelera now has over 80 employees, and their satisfaction and well-being are among Joe's highest priorities. "I'm most proud that we are able to give everyone in our organization a great place to work, a sense of family, and a sense of stability," he explains. "Our leadership team understands that every decision we make affects our employees, and so the process is very personal to us."

Joe aims to lead by example by working hard and welcoming any duty, meaningful or trivial, that comes his way. "I dread red tape and bureaucracy," he says. "It is important to me to make decisions rapidly and move constantly because this keeps us at the front of the pack. If you overanalyze, you quickly fall behind. I'm more of a free-form thinker."

This effective free-form thinking paired with an impeccable work ethic perhaps stem from his childhood days, when his father would turn any common household chore into a job that corresponded to some form of compensation. "My father did this to help me understand that results and rewards follow accomplishments," Joe explains. "My parents were both extremely hard workers, and I definitely absorbed that trait from them."

His father's early lessons in cause and effect sparked an entrepreneurial flame in young Joe that transformed the terrain of his days and experience, as he was constantly mowing lawns, helping friends fix their bikes, or performing odd jobs around the neighborhood and then asking others if they needed similar services. "I was always anxious to take an ideal or opportunity and figure out how I could make it lucrative," he remembers. "If one neighbor needed help spring cleaning, odds were that others could use that service as well, and I would pursue that. I liked work—it was not so much about money, but more about accomplishing the goal. Money comes and goes, but finding that next opportunity was what drove me and really interested me." Joe was also compelled by the acquisition of knowledge, as the odd jobs he engaged in almost always resulted in the development of a new interpersonal skill or expertise that he wouldn't have acquired otherwise.

In advising young entrepreneurs entering the business world today, Joe stresses the importance of geography when it comes to accessing opportunity. "If you're from a small town and you're looking for a career without ceilings, move someplace where there's a thriving economy," he urges. "I've known so many smart people who will never have the opportunities that will truly stretch their abilities because they'll always stay in the same small town they grew up in. Don't be afraid to make the move and chase your dream to some crazy location if you have to."

Beyond location, Joe explains the importance of feeling out a career that truly accesses one's skill set. "Look beyond the traditional boundaries that are put in front of you and try to figure out what fits your personality and strengths best," he suggests. "Don't be constrained by traditional job types, but try to imagine the future opportunities in your chosen field that might not exist yet. Look for industries at the brink of blossoming, or industries that have some long-term growth pattern," he continues.

In examining Accelera's history and success, we readily see these words brought to life in Joe's own ability to forecast the coming trends in the technology industry, and his willingness to take risks has translated this ability into a legacy that is tangible, compelling, and evolving. His nuanced understanding of how technology and markets work in tandem are what brought Accelera to where it is today, and they will certainly keep the organization poised at the forefront of its industry in years to come.

Bill Carteaux

The Go-Getter's Way

"You didn't just hit it out of the park, you hit it out of the universe," came the headhunter's voice over the phone.

The higher-ups at Van Dorn, now Demag Plastics Group, had originally told Bill Carteaux that they were not going to entertain any internal candidates to fill the vacant position of President and CEO of the Americas. "If you want an opportunity, you're going to have to convince our CEO in Germany that you're capable of doing this," they had told him. After traveling to Germany only to have the CEO cancel their meeting, Bill then pulled a series of maneuvers to obtain a twenty-minute window with the man several days later, which proved enough to get his name thrown in the hat. Maximizing his nuanced knowledge of the business through the proactive and thorough creation of a discussion document, he had come to his first interview with copies of the piece for each person at the meeting. The document had predicted the questions of the interviewers to a tee, winning him the position over 28 other candidates worldwide. "No one else was close," he was told. You can bet that, when it came to dogged determination, no one else came close either.

If one were to talk to the people who knew Bill when he was young, they would tell you he was always in charge. Born the youngest of four children and raised in a small farming community in northeast Indiana, it was almost as if the renowned Midwestern work ethic had been ingrained in his soul long before he got his first job at the age of fourteen bailing hay for a buck an hour for the preacher across the road. Now President and CEO of the SPI Plastics Industry Trade Association, Bill's journey is a testament not so much to being in charge, but to *taking* charge, living with a fierce perseverance that has carried him to where he is today.

SPI is the largest plastics trade association in the country and represents the broad interest of the entire industry, uniting material suppliers, processors, moldmakers, and equipment manufacturers throughout the entire value chain of the industry. Advocacy remains a primary focus of the organization as it targets plastic-specific federal issues as well as tax and healthcare-related work coalitions. In this capacity, SPI is recognized as the preeminent organization worldwide for working on food contact plastic applications with the FDA. Their influence extends laterally to state activity through the determination of public policy, as well as internationally to address trade issues that specifically impact the plastics industry.

Beyond advocacy, SPI also focuses on communications and marketing within the industry regarding the industry, now aiming to extend these lines of communication externally to the general public as well. This plethora of efforts is punctuated by SPI's ownership and management of various trade shows and conferences throughout the year, with its centerpiece being the triennial occurrence of the largest plastics trade show in the Western Hemisphere. The show traditionally umbrellas one million square feet of exhibition space and 70,000 attendees from around the world assembling to buy, sell, explore, and admire all that the plastics industry has to offer.

As has been the case with so many business sectors, the past several years have wrought difficult and unpredictable conditions for the plastics industry—a period that may have spelled out the end for SPI, were it not for Bill's experience and leadership. He remembers a particularly adrenaline-pumping period beginning in February of 2009, when large blocks of exhibitors began to consider withdrawing from the trade show scheduled only several short months later. Instead of watching the association's opus unravel before his eyes, Bill hopped a plane to Japan within a week to meet with the key exhibitors that collectively controlled 55 percent of the injection molding market in the U.S. With a persistence that refused to take no for an answer, he eventually met with each industry leader, developing friendships and collecting information to assist in molding his next move.

After learning that Japanese sales were down 90 percent and later receiving a call that the European exhibitors were also planning to pull out of the show, Bill spent the following two weeks working with his officer group to develop a stimulus package. The committee approved the plan with no discussion of how to fund the $3+ million package, save for a single comment: "I'm not worried; Bill will figure out how to make this work." Later that month, Bill presented the finance committee with a plan for a much-needed restructuring of the organization such that the package could be covered, and he met with each of the association's thirty board members over the next several months to gain support. "I learned a lot during that time, selling my concepts across a broad range of people to get the approval we needed to move forward," he reflects. "My sales background really compels me to communicate with people throughout the entire course of an issue and negotiation, allowing me to fully understand what the issue is and gain an educated idea of how to solve it."

Through his efforts to provide subsidization to exhibitors and allow free admission to attendees, the 2009 trade show proved a ray of light amidst otherwise dark times, marking a turning point in the industry for which people are still thanking Bill today. "We can't know what could have happened to the industry had the show fallen through," Bill comments. "All we know is what *did* happen." Though their overall attendance was down 30 percent, unique company representation was only down 12 percent. The attendees that did show up were the buyers of their organizations, and as a result of the slimmer crowd, sellers were able to spend more quality one-on-one time with customers. In fact, the main Japanese seller sold more machines at the 2009 show than at any other year—a testament not only to the efforts of the association itself, but to the pure power of ingenuity to triumph in the face of adversity.

When examining the personal history behind Bill's unique go-getter mentality, one can readily identify both innate inclination and cultivated learning at work. Bill had actually intended to pursue a career as an automotive mechanic in high school, but after gaining ample dealership experience, he felt as though life might have something else in store for him. "I couldn't see myself doing it forever; I had bigger aspirations," he recalls. His parents didn't have the money to send him to college, so he joined the air force to get an education but soon received an honorable discharge from basic training due to a previous detached retina. Disappointed but not discouraged, he decided to pay for college himself. "I knew the only thing I could ultimately control was my own action," he says now. "I may not be the smartest guy in the room, but I had been told that drive and determination win out over raw brains any day."

With this in mind, he enrolled at Purdue University in Fort Wayne, working at a gas station and car wash in his spare time and befriending a man by the name of Bill Dice. The two shared a passion for cars and would talk avidly about them every Saturday until Bill transferred to Purdue's main campus for his junior and senior year.

The experience of campus life transformed Bill in ways that proved to be as invaluable as they were drastic. It was almost as if his innate fortes for leadership and strategy had lain dormant, waiting for the right environment to set them aflame. Mirroring his father's passion and commitment to community involvement in many ways, Bill attended summer conferences for the Trade Association, joined the American Society of Agricultural Engineers, and served as Vice Chair of its National Student chapter. Bill not only came into his own as a student leader, but also as a family man, marrying a woman named Sherri the summer before his senior year.

His innovation skills were further honed after college while working for the Indiana Farm Bureau Co-op, excelling through a state-operated fast-track management program and thoroughly immersing himself in dairy farm culture. He then made a considerable stir in the industry by endorsing and selling new technology that proved to increase milk production by 25 percent. "The whole experience taught me the importance and profitability of always looking at new technology or new ways of accomplishing things, never being constrained by the status quo," he explains.

Several years out of college and amidst this success, Bill found himself covering an emergency shift at the old gas station where he had worked throughout his youth, when suddenly his old friend Bill Dice showed up. Mr. Dice invited Bill to come work as a regional sales manager for him and wouldn't take no for an answer, so the young man took the leap of faith and never looked back. "I'm glad I did because it moved me into the industrial manufacturing side of things, setting me up for the career I have today," Bill reflects. Under the influence of a mentor and true visionary, Chet Dekko, he was thrown into any number of sink-or-swim situations in his new role, and considering he's here today to tell the tale, it's safe to assume that he succeeded in keeping his head above water. Through his efforts at assembling and implementing a strong sales team, Bill was able to quadruple the business within two years.

Despite such pronounced success, however, he knew that he needed more intensive manufacturing experience to get where he hoped to go in the future. Thus, he pursued experience in the glass industry for the next five years until Chet offered him the position of Sales Manager of their plastics machinery business, Autojectors. Bill was promoted through the ranks to President over a period of eight years, growing the business from $3.8 million to $20 million in that period.

During this time, Bill also accepted a position as VP of Marketing Van Dorn, then a $210 million company in Ohio. It was shortly after his rise to President and CEO of what had grown into a $450 million global enterprise when the former President and CEO of SPI submitted his resignation, and Bill began to receive calls encouraging him to consider the position. Though several mentors thought he was crazy to give up so much to pursue this new life, Bill has since proven that the decision was a sound one. "It has been phenomenal," he says now. "Every day has been different, and I continue to learn new things and find new ways to engage the breadth of our membership."

Yet again, Bill's decision to take this leap not only demonstrates a willingness to take risks, but also a trust in his own intuitions and inclinations that has guided him well over the years. "I have always had a good gut," Bill laughs. "Although I'm very metric-driven and analytical, I know that when my gut tells me something, the foresight is usually correct."

Beyond this insightful skill, Bill stresses the importance of developing and preserving good relationships. "Never burn any bridges," he urges. "In the business world, there have been some situations where I might have wanted to give someone a piece of my mind, only for them to later join the association, making me thankful that I had maintained good relations." Through the powerful summation of gut instinct, strong relationships, and a go-getter attitude that doesn't hear the word no, young entrepreneurs today can truly hope to create opportunities out of adversity and success out of strife.

Luke Chung

Great Risk, Greater Rewards

Luke Chung, Founder and President of Financial Modeling Specialists, Inc. (FMS) is a study in the success of taking risks. By starting FMS at the age of twenty-two and within the company's first few months bringing it to a positive cash flow level, Chung has shown how great risk can bring great reward.

Founded in 1986, FMS was originally in the business of creating financial analytical models to help organizations manage their money and control costs. Over time the company evolved into a purely software development business, branching out to not only include financial analytics but to encompass all of the data needs of their clients.

"We would help people organize their data and our focus over the years has been to help people make better decisions," Chung explains, "We organized the company into three areas of focus: products for the general public which include tools for Microsoft-related technology;

custom database applications for government and corporate solutions; and counter-terrorism and law enforcement products and services including, Sentinel Visualizer, which is a software program that helps identify hidden relationships between people, places and things that we developed in response to the challenges of the 9/11 attacks."

The idea of entrepreneurship and being in control of his own destiny has appealed to Chung his entire life. Growing up with a father who was a Land-Survey Engineer and a mother who was an Architect, Chung had self-employment modeled from birth.

"I have always admired people who could create their own businesses and lead the free enterprise system in this country. When you look at our beginnings and the people who built it, Ben Franklin and George Washington, they were inventors, farmers, and small business owners, I mean those are entrepreneurs. They didn't have a job, they created a job and they ran things. It really wasn't until the late 1800's that a large percentage of the population became employees. And so I guess I always thought that I would rather be the creator than the follower.

Even though we have a free enterprise system, probably less than five percent of the people are self-employed or are really creating their own job. Most people have jobs created by other people for them. That's not to say everyone is suited to entrepreneurship, and even those who are may not be successful. I was fortunate to have the opportunity to try it. I gave myself a year and thought I'd go to business school if I failed. It's been personally gratifying to pursue my ideas and have the market justify it financially."

Chung also became fascinated with money and how wealth grows in his early years in school. He recalls, "I remember this very distinctly, being in the seventh grade and having my math teacher compare compound interest versus simple interest. It was then that I understood why Einstein said compound interest was the greatest force in the universe."

Born the oldest son of Taiwanese immigrants, Chung learned responsibility and self-control at very young age.

"I remember that it wasn't such smooth sailing with my father when I was growing up. He and I would butt heads quite a bit. Early in my high school years, we made a deal that if I could make and keep straight A's, then there would be no rules imposed on me. If I could fulfill my "job", then there would be no curfews or discussions about my homework, but if I failed, he could dictate the rules. That was kind of entrepreneurial, and an example of how I took responsibility for myself."

Chung attended Harvard University and majored in Engineering and Physical Oceanography. Having grown up in Florida, Chung loved the ocean and had a passion for it. The major seemed like a good combination of science and real-world application of hunting or hiding submarines. But, while on a six-week research cruise off of the California coast with the Naval Postgraduate School, Chung discovered how powerful the ocean was.

"During a three day period in 20 foot seas, I vomited up and down the western seaboard and decided that I needed a career change. I wasn't spending my life doing that, no matter how fascinating it was."

This was the summer before Chung's senior year, and needing to find a career path that interested him and that he could enter with his degree was a bit challenging.

"The recruiters were on campus for positions in investment banking and management consulting, and I saw how they were using technology to manage data to make better decisions in organizations. I presented my strong analytic ability and business knowledge, and showed how that would translate to management consulting and financial analysis."

Chung was hired by Strategic Planning Associates in Washington DC, and worked for the company for two years before focusing entirely his own company in 1987.

"I understood that there were several avenues for the generation of revenue for a business. You can sell your time and for every hour that you work you get some compensation (whether that is minimum wage or the top rate earned by the best lawyer in town), but at some point you are limited by the number of hours you can work and the amount that you can charge per hour; you can make money with money as in compound interest or investments; you can create something or invent something that could be sold over and over again to generate some sort of intellectual property stream (independent of the hours that your putting in); and lastly you can sell other people's time. The main point is to not have one's time be the factor or limitation of one's revenue when creating a company."

After twenty-five years, FMS has reached new heights in the technology industry and in its own history. FMS products have over 50,000 customers in 100 countries, their Sentinel Visualizer program led to an investment by InQTel, the CIA's venture capital fund, and they have created a wide range of custom solutions that impact lives and the way people operate. Examples include a solution for the six United Nations (UN) agencies and the Pan-American Health Organization to coordinate logistics for natural disaster relief efforts in over 80 countries. They've also created a solution to manage the operations of the Washington Speakers Bureau, the world's premier lecture agency, and many other solutions for non-profits, small businesses, government agencies, and large organizations.

FMS has weathered the storm of a tumultuous industry. "We've been through multiple business and technology cycles over the last 25 years. People forget that we started in a DOS world, which turned into Windows, then web, and recently added mobility and cloud.

There are many organizations that we've partnered or worked for that no longer exist. Think about this recession that recently came through and people were complaining that the economy shrunk a few percent, maybe. We are involved in an industry where eco-systems, just disappear. The DOS market disappeared and went to Windows. The dot.com boom and bust just took out a lot of companies. So having the economy shrink just a couple of percent is not significant in comparison.

We have experienced great years in a terrible economy and terrible years in a great economy. Our industry isn't tied to the GNP. We are a little company that can live or die based on having one good contract or losing one big contract."

Chung, a father of two young girls, not only cares about the success of his business and the employees found within it, but he also has a vision for the future of the world and how he can utilize the technology available, and develop new technologies, to help make the world a better place.

"I love creating things that have never been done before, so there is an inventor part of me that needs to be fulfilled."

Chung also works with several organizations to utilize his unique combination of skills and experience to mentor and educate the next generation.

"I work with the Network for Teaching Entrepreneurship and went into the classroom at Annandale High School last year. I also serve on a Business and Community Advisory Board to the Superintendent of Schools and serve on the IT Policy Advisory Committee to Fairfax County Board of Supervisors representing the School Board."

Chung's advice to recent college graduates is to pursue their passions. "There are so many opportunities in the world but the world doesn't come to you to tell you what you should do. It's your responsibility to figure out what you want to do, then pursue opportunities in that space. If it's something you're passionate about, then it's not a job. Being young offers to opportunity to take risks that are minimal over a lifetime but offer the opportunity to change the course of your whole life."

Certainly a visionary, and taker of risks, Luke Chung has proven, at a young age, that you make your own destiny and that great rewards await those willing to take the chance.

David Dacquino

Embracing the Summit

When David Dacquino arrived home in Tucson, Arizona, from a business trip in Chile, he was expecting his workweek to resume its typical demanding yet fulfilling pace. What he couldn't have guessed, however, was that his life was about to acquire a new dimension—one that would take his understanding of "demanding yet fulfilling" to new heights, both literally and metaphorically.

"I've signed you up for that mountain climb you wanted to do, and you start with your trainer tomorrow morning at the gym," said his wife, Mary.

Several months earlier, Dave had overheard a discussion between family friends about summiting Mount Rainier and receiving their mountain climbing certification. Employed by Raytheon Missile Systems at the time, his job delivered considerable mental challenges yet made no physical demands of him, and as he was constantly seeking such demands in other aspects of his life, his interest had been immediately piqued. He had set the possibility on the backburner, however, until Mary had so graciously, if not unexpectedly, brought it back to the forefront of his attention with her announcement.

True to form and never one to shy from a challenge, Dave showed up for his first day of training the next morning, and in no time he had completed the rigorous course. He did indeed summit Mount Rainier, earning his official certification and, in the process, cementing what would become a lifelong love of mountain climbing that would not only characterize his capacity for personal and physical greatness, but for professional magnitude as well.

"The sport challenges me physically, emotionally, mentally, and spiritually—it's all-encompassing, and in that, it's perfect for me," he gushes today. The true breadth and scope of this challenge is epitomized by the time he climbed Aconcagua, the highest peak in the Americas. "During that climb, I hit a wall and couldn't go any further," he recalls. "I was emotionally wracked, physically empty, and scared. Somehow, though, I broke through that wall, eliciting a euphoric feeling the likes of which I had never experienced. Finding the inner strength to see that a perceived wall isn't really a wall was a true lesson in mind over matter—an idea which I had never truly ascribed to before. Ever since then, when my work gets me down, I use this lesson to recalibrate, reset my footing, and drive forward." Now the CEO of the U.S. company VT Group, owned by Babcock International Group, a UK-based company specializing in military support contract work, Dave continues to use his strength of character to summit any challenge, be it business or geological.

The VT Group actually began as two collections of shipbuilders, Vosper and Thornycroft, which came together under the Royal Navy of the United Kingdom 150 years ago. As maritime legend has it, the group eventually permeated the larger shipbuilding and modification industry and then later migrated further into the services business.

Moving out of the maritime sector and into critical asset management, the VT Group assumed maintenance of all vehicles for the London metropolitan police, decommissioned nuclear submarines, and retired nuclear facilities throughout the UK. Beyond such sophisticated and complex critical asset management responsibilities, the business assumed an educational role as well, including the training of BMW mechanics and of army, navy, and air force personnel.

This broad spectrum of services was lent new expanse ten years ago, when the VT Group began acquiring companies in the U.S. This intercontinental endeavor began with the purchase of Griffin, an infrastructure management company that maintains the King's Bay nuclear submarine base on the Southern East Coast. They also manage NASA's launch facility on the East Coast, as well as Fort Huachuca, where U.S. Government unmanned aircraft are maintained and tested. VT then bought Milcom, a C4I communication control computer company that works on maritime, nuclear submarine, and surface ships. Through this acquisition, VT assumed upgrade responsibilities of communications and self defense systems for the U.S. Navy and now augments those services with physical security and healthcare IT as well. Finally, VT made its third major purchase, AEPCO. In this acquisition, VT works for the Army Materiel Command handling an array of rotary wing aviation logistics challenges from maintenance assessment to field oil analysis. Last year, under Dave's leadership, VT Group acquired an unmanned aircraft services business. Today, VT's U.S. business is a half-billion dollar operation with a workforce approaching two thousand five hundred.

When VT Group first came knocking on Dave's door, he had spent 27 years working in large U.S. corporations and was situated well at Raytheon. VT was headquartered in Alpharetta, GA, at the time, and had issued a mandate to consolidate its three companies into one major operation while looking for additional acquisitions and continuing to grow the business, evolving into new markets while exiting others where the company seemed to have run its course. Dave initially declined, opting instead to stay with Raytheon, which boasted more internal mobility and greater access to resources and assets. When VT came knocking a second time, however, Dave utilized his mountaineering mindset to recalibrate and reconsider. "After meeting with the UK leadership team, I became excited about their vision and where they wanted to go," Dave remembers. "I recognized a unique opportunity to guide and shape the culture of the U.S. operation from its fledgling stages according to that vision and through my own experiences. I would have the leeway to instill the better features of a big company while leaving the bureaucracy out of the blueprint, and I found a certain thrill in the prospect of that challenge."

Why did VT set its sights on Dave? An aeronautic engineer by education, he had spent many years on the aircraft manufacturing side of aviation but had also accumulated nuanced experience in the services side. "With my dual background in service and U.S. defense, VT also appreciated the aggressive currents of my character and forecasted the ways in which I would be able to change the markets of the company," he reflects. "Moving into the U.S. was a bold move for VT, and some of the acquisitions hadn't been targeted exactly right, so they were looking for major changes. I knew it would be a formidable task—despite this fact, or maybe *because* of this fact, my wife and I decided it would be a good fit for me. Though the revenue size was a third of what I had handled at Raytheon, the challenge was much broader, and I had total ownership reporting to a Board. It was an opportunity to stretch my wings and realize my full potential, and it was a great decision for me."

Dave had always wanted to be a pilot, but when he graduated from Farmingdale University flight school in 1978 into an economy where most pilots were out of work, he realized he may need a Plan B. This realization was seconded by one of his professors when he began studying at Arizona State, who said he should consider engineering as a backup. As luck would have it, he realized an immediate affinity for the industry, and he was promptly hired by Lockheed upon finishing school to build aircraft in Burbank, California. Seven years later, he transferred within the company to Ontario, California, where he transitioned into the services side in the deployment of the aircraft. "It was in the midst of the Cold War, and I had entered into an aspect of the business where you really get your fingernails dirty, sending people into harm's way on missions throughout the Soviet Union," Dave reflects. He also worked special operations for C130s, and such aircraft played pivotal rolls in operations like Kosovo and Kuwait.

After this period, Dave was advised that he would benefit from learning the electronics side of the business, so he worked for a business in New Hampshire before making his fourth move to Lockheed in South Carolina where he would lead the consolidation of the company's aeronautical support services. Still drawn to the services side of the business, however, he then transitioned over to Raytheon Missile Systems in Tucson and then to Raytheon Technical Services back on the East Coast, from whence he made the leap to VT.

"I think the swift forward motion of my professional evolution was fueled in large part by my willingness to take on some of the uglier jobs," Dave reveals today. "For instance, I remember a time when Lockhead was trying to budget, calculate, and figure out how much it would cost to deploy people as part of one of our assignments. The government needed financial forecasts of what it would cost to do so, but none of us knew how to provide those. Still, I raised my hand and volunteered to take on the learning curve. This got me into the financial side of the business and helped me to understand contracts."

Taking on such challenges augmented Dave's engineering background with an understanding of the financial side of the business, and this expertise was further enhanced down the road when he earned his MBA. "My willingness to be versatile and to talk several different languages lent me a skill set that afforded me opportunities that others didn't have," he recognizes today.

Beyond these hard skills, Dave also strove to acquire and practice wisdom from mentors and role models whenever he could. "One mentor taught me to never let anyone get between you and your customer, and to never insulate yourself," he remembers. "I also learned not to take myself too seriously. These lessons served me very well moving forward. I made sure I was always walking the floor, getting to know the people I was working with and really understanding what the business was." Acquiring this level of diversity, both in understanding people and in understanding the job, propelled Dave forward and was vital in realizing the success he's attained today for VT.

Of all these successes, however, Dave holds that his ability to put his ego aside and utilize a collaborative leadership and problem solving philosophy is among his greatest triumphs. "So many of us have been taught in the past that a dictatorial decisiveness is the way of business—that, as leaders, we must take the data, make a decision, and march," Dave explains. "But this isn't how business works today, and it doesn't work with a diverse workforce. Young people are learning and responding differently; therefore, we as leaders must motivate differently, and being collaborative is the way to do this."

This lesson, unsurprisingly, ties directly into the experience of mountain climbing that has so profoundly shaped Dave's professional endurance. "Climbing teaches you about following just as much as it teaches you about leading," he explains. "When you're hanging from a rope at 20,000 feet and tied to other people, you care very deeply about their successes or failures because you're one millisecond behind them, whichever direction they end up going. You and your team must act as one organism, just as it is in the most successful corporate teams. Each team member must actively participate in following and leading, and you can't be a good leader unless you're a good follower."

This balance, as invaluable to the lives of mountain climbers as it is to the lives of companies, should be embraced by any young entrepreneur entering the business world today. Adverse and mountainous terrain is inevitable in any life of ambition, yet approaching adversity with a sound mental physique and an immovable inner conviction allows one to embrace any summit, personal or professional, with the courage and perseverance it takes to succeed.

BERNHARDT

WEALTH MANAGEMENT

James DeBardelaben

The Path Beyond the Wall

If you're a special operations soldier on the ground in an expeditionary environment like Afghanistan, your goal is to be invisible. To save your own life, you must know what's going on around you: a key turning in the ignition of a vehicle located a thousand meters away, a generator rumbling off, a whispered message through a communication device. Who are they? Where are they? Where are they going? Your survival hangs in the balance of leveraging such information.

James DeBardelaben has made it his life's work to provide the answers to these very questions. As the President and CEO of IvySys Technologies, LLC, he understands the seminal importance of situational awareness for troops on the ground in unfamiliar and possibly hostile territory. He understands it so well, in fact, that he built a company to address this very issue.

IvySys Technologies is a networked intelligence, surveillance, and reconnaissance (ISR) company providing solutions and services to our nation's defense and intelligence community, developing advanced collection, processing, exploitation, and dissemination systems for ISR applications. Their core competence lies in developing and mapping advanced signal processing algorithms to high performance architectures that make it possible to conduct highly advanced computations within a comparatively small and portable device.

James first got the idea for these devices from the video game industry, which relies heavily upon a technology called graphics processing units (GPUs), designed to interpret data into an incredible visual experience. IvySys repurposes GPUs to interpret data coming from sensors platforms. This super computer-like performance allows IvySys to process the data at near real-time speeds and turn it into actionable intelligence for the soldier or analyst in the field.

With a father who worked as a dispatcher for Santa Fe Railroad and a mother who worked as a law firm billing analyst, James grew up in Chicago amidst modest circumstances and did not, as a child, dream that he would end up where he is today. He attended Mendel Catholic High School, an all African American environment that enforced a strict dress code and sent 90 percent of its graduates to college. "It ingrained in me the idea that people will take you more seriously if you take your business seriously," he reminisces. "Thus, we always dress in business attire at IvySys." His first job was a summer experience at Argonne National Laboratory where he had the opportunity to work with a different scientist each day. "The teachers at Mendel were really invested in us, and I think that makes all the difference now," he affirms.

James first entered the defense marketplace as a program manager at the Johns Hopkins University Applied Physics Laboratory (JHU/APL), where he ran special operations ISR programs focusing on persistent surveillance. In this capacity, he worked to develop portable, battery-powered sensors that could be left behind at the sites at which they gathered surveillance. James, however, found himself wanting something more. "The role of the lab [JHU/APL] has traditionally been to serve as a trusted agent for the government, not to go build fieldable operational prototypes," he remembers. "I could see that there was a lot of opportunity for a smaller company to come in with something agile that wasn't tied to past technology and could really leverage everything that's out there today."

It is upon this philosophy that IvySys was built, and it is with this goal in mind that it operates today. Always exploring the newest, hot-off-the-shelf commercially available technology and what new capabilities it might impart, James and his team know what their competition is doing and how to supersede it.

Well equipped with a strong working knowledge of small unit operations and ISR technologies, James left Johns Hopkins in March of 2006 and launched IvySys just two days later when he began consulting for the Defense Advanced Research Projects Agency (DARPA), providing subject matter expertise. "The true genesis of IvySys came when I was providing consulting expertise for the program managers there," James recalls. "During that period, I had the opportunity to see the vast diversity of approaches and problems that the war fighter faces. It was then that I realized the hardest problem was not getting the data, but rather processing that data fast enough to provide the war fighter with actionable intelligence." In 2008, with this challenge in mind, he began assembling a team of individuals with finely honed and unique capabilities that were mutually complementary so as to best examine this challenge from every possible angle.

Delaying his first hire until this time allowed James to self-fund the company, and throughout those first years, he would wait to make a new hire until his most recent hire was picked up by a contract. Though this interval was never very long, James approached a point where he realized he wanted to manage growth in a different manner. With this in mind, he learned the art of building a core team that could scale according to the amount of work that was demanded. With the accounting, business development, marketing, human resources, recruiting, and management teams in place, IvySys was equipped with the tools and processes needed to expand from 10 to 100 employees at the drop of a hat, rendering it a strong competitor in the defense marketplace.

Since its inception, IvySys has grown 300 percent annually in revenues, drawing between $3.5 and $4 million in 2009 with 15 employees. James is now looking to the upcoming years and considering how he can engender more explosive growth as the industry around him changes. "A number of the procurements are shifting from a cost plus fixed fee model to a fixed price model, which means that, as a small company, we have to approach customers with fieldable technology as opposed to just the plans for that technology," he explains. "Our clients are no longer funding us to produce an idea; rather, we must come with an actual product, which involves a considerable investment up front."

However, just as it specializes in situational awareness for troops, IvySys maintains its own unique and comprehensive situational awareness of the changing terrain of its industry and has no doubt that it, too, will maneuver such variables with success. "We're currently positioning ourselves to grow five-fold within the next three years," James reports. "After growing by word-of-mouth and referrals throughout the first several years, I've learned that having a business development pipeline in place is critical. We now have a customer base into which we're constantly feeding new ideas."

James received an undergraduate degree in electrical engineering from Brown University and a master's in the same field from Princeton, though his time at Princeton was intended to go towards a PhD instead. "I had joined Princeton's PhD program because people said I was good enough to do it, but not necessarily because I was driven to do it," he reflects now. It wasn't until he left Princeton and cultivated his own inner drive that he realized the monumental importance of choosing one's path for one's own self instead of for others. "I then got my PhD from Georgia Tech, and my mindset was completely different," he continues. "I knew why I was there—I wanted to chart some new territory, and I was trying to optimize my own particular career path. You need some real mental toughness to get through that, and this toughness must come from within."

Now that he's leading a team and a business, James has aimed to inspire this same mental toughness in his staff members, motivating them to grind through a project and move forward as a unit. In doing this, he reflects back to his high school days when he ran on the track team. "We wanted, collectively, to be the best runners, and we pushed each other everyday," he recalls fondly. "Even if we had one guy come in first and another come in 100th, we treated it as though the whole team had come in 100th. We ran as a pack, never leaving anyone behind, and this mindset stays with me today."

During those long and arduous track practices, James's coach used to say that, whenever a runner felt as though he had hit a wall, he still had 33 percent left to give. James has since applied this philosophy to all areas of his life, using the formula to help him persevere even when he has felt at his most taxed.

In advising young entrepreneurs entering the business world today, James stresses the importance of pursuing advanced degrees and planning ahead. "Look at your end goal and then assess which of your opportunities will build the skill set you need to move forward and develop the relationships you need to achieve that goal," he advises. "The longer you're away from an academic environment, the harder it is to return to it, so start planning now. Now is the best time of any."

But how, exactly, does one determine this end goal? James credits his time at Brown with the expansion of his conceptualization of his own potential, thanks to the diversity he encountered there. "I was exposed to students from all over and from a wide range of economic backgrounds, and all this variance compelled me to envision the concept of a career path from all different angles," he describes. "I learned how to visualize my own end goal from the people that surrounded me, utilizing these different perspectives to choose which was the best one for me."

Whether he's breaking through a wall of exhaustion by applying the 33 percent rule, or breaking through a wall of public opinion by identifying and pursuing his own path, James is a testament to the transient nature of limitations. In fact, he feels that his best decision was born from the adversity he faced in attempting to earn his PhD at Princeton. "Instead of giving up, I kept pressing forward and didn't accept the school's assessment," he points out. "Because of that decision, things began to fall into place. I got into an even better school of engineering, I received a teaching assistantship that paid for my tuition, and I later received other research assistantships and fellowships. In fact, it was through Georgia Tech that I accumulated many of the resources and connections that made IvySys possible."

Though the act of pursuing his PhD figured prominently in the development of IvySys, James emphasizes that it doesn't take a PhD to do what he does, nor does it require one to be successful. Rather, he stresses that each person has the liberty and agency to build their own path toward achieving the end goal of a successful and fulfilling life—there is no set way of doing things. "I'd personally like to see other minorities with similar backgrounds realize that a path to success like this as a real, viable option for them," says James. "To believe in yourself is far better than believing what other people are telling you."

Though daring to follow your own unique path inevitably means you will run into your own unique walls, making the commitment to break through these walls is the only way to ensure that your path will continue far beyond them.

Diana Dibble

Those That Never Give Up

In 2001, already a 14-year veteran of the federal procurement arena, Diana Dibble was primed for a new beginning. She and her future business partner Molly Gimmel would resign from their positions at Deloitte and Touche at the end of the business day to found Design To Delivery Inc, or D2DInc, a small firm specializing in procurement support services for government contractors. Diana had a strong history in government contracting services, expertise, knowledge, and a pool of promised and potential clients. The date was September 10.

"We all know what happened the next day," says Diana. "The world was losing its mind. My mom said, 'The whole world is falling apart, and you just left your job.' I had a thousand dollar a month mortgage and a day-old government contracting start-up in an environment of serious uncertainty." Still, Diana wasn't concerned. For those that never give up, failure doesn't have a chance to appear on the horizon.

Indeed, she had good reason to be confident. She had a firm grasp of the ebb and flow of demand from the government for contracting services, and how the timing of world events such as geopolitical conflicts and the transition into a new presidential administration affected that demand. Connecting defense contractors to the Department of Defense was one of many specialties at D2DInc, and they immersed themselves in that sector.

There was another reason D2DInc was able to succeed in volatile times, why it was from its inception well-positioned in terms of its client-base, and why it is still today driven to be a market leader in government contracting services. There may have been no marketing performed before the foundation of the firm on September 10th, but Diana and this industry go way back.

Diana's first experience with government contracting was while working for a uniform contractor, R&R Uniforms, in the late 80s. "I was an admin (administrative assistant)," Diana says with a laugh. She was also pursuing her MBA at night school, her previous experience being a BFA in musical theatre from Syracuse University and in a retail buying office for Garfinkel's. The uniform contractor loved that Diana had retail experience, and it wasn't long before her boss gave her the opportunity to bid her first contract, solo. She quickly took the initiative to bid on janitorial uniforms solicitation, a $90 thousand contract. She won. According to Diana, the feeling of that first big win was "dangerous," and she was immediately hooked.

"I liked this winning stuff," Diana recalls. "It was fun." Her boss at R&R was an ex-government employee person and she was willing to share her knowledge with Diana. She was the first of several mentors from diverse contracting backgrounds that set off this mad dash of Diana's that has yet to slacken as she continues to learn and master the entire territory of government contracting.

"The people I've worked with over the years have been amazing and really willing to share," Diana says, and not just about contracting.

"I was listening to anything they were willing to show me how to do," she continues. She was able to serve as a Facility Security Officer, get a clearance, and learn about those security protocols; she worked as director of human resources and took classes on the logistics and legalities of hiring and firing; she learned how to price contracts by working with that company's CFO; she even made sure to understand such office infrastructures as servers and network connections. "I would not be where I am today if people hadn't been willing to help me," she says now.

It is precisely this inner recognition of how much help she's received that drives her to give back today. In fact, D2DInc has a strong internship program that has even led to full-time hires. "We try to bring interns in and give them opportunities," she says. While most people think of internships as answering the phone and fetching coffee, interning at D2DInc is far from that. "When an intern comes to us, we have them helping us with doing work for our own business development activities and reviewing our proposals," Diana explains. In this way, D2DInc not only contributes to those eager to learn, like Diana herself was, but also benefits the firm in a real and meaningful way. D2DInc also hires young people directly out of college and trains them, filling a need at the firm while providing opportunities. "I learned to do this because I experienced how pivotal this help can be, first at R&R and then everywhere else," she explains.

After a year at the uniform company and then taking a year off for full-time MBA studies, she was hired in 1990 as an administrative assistant for Pepsi-Cola of Washington, DC, but was quickly promoted to marketing/public relations/special events manager. After that, she accepted a position at Shepard-Patterson where she worked for almost three and a half years until 1995, once again wearing many hats and supporting multiple departments. It was around this time, in 1994, that she started her first company part-time. Later name *dCUBED* (after her initials—her first married name was Duke), she went full-time with the endeavor in 1996 after being laid off from a marketing support director position. She then put dCUBED on hold for a year when she went to work for Deloitte, later bringing it back into the spotlight and merging it with D2DInc after that enterprise was launched.

According to Diana, it is this diversely practical education that allows her and D2DInc to not merely specialize in narrow bands of the procurement process, but to offer a start-to-finish service that is atypical for her firm's size, with unrivaled know-how. "Well, my education and Molly," she corrects herself.

Diana first met Molly Gimmel at Deloitte in 2000, and from the beginning they knew how well they could work together, seeing eye-to-eye on everything from government contracts to the value of hard work. Friends and colleagues have commented about Diana and Molly that they owe some of their success as a partnership to their gender. Whether that's true or not, Diana laughs, "We work things out instead of going out back and beating the crap out of each other."

"Between Molly and me," she says, "we know just about everything in this business." Molly's a Generation Xer, but Diana accepts her as an honorary fellow-boomer. "She has boomer qualities," she says. "She's in the club."

An orthodox Jew, Diana says that God has been the most influential force in her life, and she believes that her strong ethical foundation provides a firm basis for her personal success. "Even as a young child, that's been something very important to me," she says. "I base how I deal with people on values I've taken from a religious perspective, like being fair and ethical." When things aren't going right, she explains, it is through her faith that she can take a personal inventory, discover herself, and get that wake-up call to take a step back and address the problem.

This ethical grounding has also directly contributed to the well-being of her business. "Sometimes we've said to a client, 'Don't bid on something, because you can't win it,' knowing that's something out of our pocket, but knowing still more that it's the right thing to do," Diana affirms. Clients respond to that, but she emphasizes that her philosophy is not necessarily a business strategy. "We do what we think is right," she says, "and we do what will help our clients the most, and that comes back to benefit us." Thanks to this mindset, Diana has few regrets, and she believes the greatest times for D2DInc are yet to come.

These good times will certainly be optimized by the many lessons Diana and Molly have learned so far, especially in terms of personnel management. "I do think we were reluctant to lay anyone off at the downturn, and that cost us financially," Diana acknowledges. She saw a need to keep the team intact and had plenty of business pending, but she admits now that in some cases it would have been better for the company and often for the employees themselves for them to adjust the size of the enterprise appropriate to the economic climate. "After all," Diana says, "if the company suffers and can't sustain the same number of people, whom am I really benefiting by keeping us at that level of personnel?"

Looking back at D2DInc's history not only inspires lessons, however, but also marvels. By Diana's account, the September 11th attacks and the ensuing changes drastically altered the face of government contracting in America. Ultimately it was a favorable time to start D2DInc, and Diana thinks they have been able to do great work, not just for the success of their own company but also for the security of the country as a whole in doing their part to make their clients successful and carry the economy forward.

"There are many small businesses in defense contracting who perhaps wouldn't have been able to get into the industry if we hadn't had the opportunity to work with them and help those companies respond to what was suddenly happening in the world," Diana says. "In that sense, we had a hand in helping our country be safe and are very grateful to have been able to give back in such a meaningful way."

With a firm grasp on the historical context within which they find themselves, Diana, Molly and their team are now on the lookout for the next role they'll assume as a market leader. "We have a great uniqueness in that we are relatively small, and yet we offer complete start-to-finish support in an industry that can overly fragment the procurement process," she points out. Diana's current challenge expands even beyond the boundaries of the business to include other opportunities she hopes to optimize as well, such as completing the writing of the book on government contracting that she's been working on for a few years now. "I have several sections written," she says. "It's a challenge to keep up with changing regulations and the breakneck-pace work environment we keep going on around here, but I am constantly having new ideas and I'd like to get them all down in a way that is relevant to people."

Until then, she's chasing after her next great decision and not focused on limiting herself to any set legacy just yet. "I care about my family, my husband's children and my grandchildren. They're my legacy," she affirms. "I'm proud that Molly and I have kept our business together through this downturn, and despite some moments of real uncertainty, we have really stood up to it and kept this going. That is what I'm most proud of. That we refuse to give up."

David M. Doggette

A Spirit-Filled Success

When David Doggette agreed to play the piano during a scholarship ceremony for Howard County in his hometown of Columbia, Maryland, he declined compensation, interested only in whether he would be randomly selected as one of the winning students. His odds were one in two. When the night ended and his name had not been called, the disappointment shone on his face. Sometimes, though, it would seem that life presents us with small setbacks only to place us on the path leading to our greatest victories.

The woman who had requested the grace of his musical ability was quite dismayed at the outcome of the lottery, so when she ran across a notice for another scholarship, David's name was the first thing that came to mind. The National Security Agency (NSA) was essentially employing a select number of students to attend undergraduate curriculums in computer science, math, engineering, and foreign language through a scholarship that covered tuition, books, room, and board, and David decided to apply. He was one of five students to be selected out of 50, and with that, he finished out one year at Oakwood College in Huntsville, Alabama, and transferred to Stanford University.

"To me, that was a miracle in itself and completely changed my outlook on life," David marvels today. Now the CEO of 2HB Software Designs, he credits this fundamental turning point in his life as the initial awakening of the entrepreneurial spirit within.

2HB provides consulting services with an emphasis on software engineering, systems engineering, management consulting, information security, web based development, and telecommunications systems and services. Though their knowledge base is centered strongly on the Department of Defense, the company is slated to expand to serve other federal agencies in the near future, with the possibility of participation in commercial endeavors down the road.

David first met his business partner, Reginald Hay, at Stanford, where he was participating in the NSA scholarship program as well. The two graduated in 1991 and commenced fulfilling their four-and-a-half year work commitment to NSA, but this did not stop them from exploring other career horizons as well. "I had just earned my first master's degree in computer science, and starting our own company sounded like a novel idea," David remembers. "We had knowledge that people found extremely useful." Thus, 2HB was launched in David's townhouse in 1994 and was open for business in the evenings when the young entrepreneurs returned home after their nine-to-fives. Their first contract was the coding of a PC-based software application to work on a Mac, teaching mathematics to second and third grade students using prominent minority figures in history.

David didn't start working full-time for 2HB until 1998, when the small company was contracted to develop a 30,000 line Java application that utilized cutting edge technology to generate major monthly reports for the Department of Defense. The project went well, but faced with dismal Federal budget cuts for fiscal year 2000, David and Reginald noted that the funding for both of their contracts had been reallocated. Acting pragmatically, the two decided to put 2HB on hold, shutting the enterprise down from 2000 to 2003. "We had enough confidence in ourselves to know that we were going to open up shop again when the time was right," David reflects now.

"That interim was a perfect litmus test for identifying the entrepreneurial bug," he continues. "When people would ask me what I did for a living, I found it exceptionally difficult to answer. When you've got that bug and are used to owning your own business, it really does a number when you have to say you work for someone else." With this in mind, David leapt at the first opportunity to return his focus to 2HB.

When Reginald agreed to meet David at a Thai restaurant in Virginia in September of 2003, David was ready. The tragic events of 9/11 were still reverberating throughout the nation, funneling money back into the intelligence community and presenting new opportunities for contractors to serve the government in its time of need. With such a textured history in that community, David and Reginald seemed ideally equipped to meet this challenge. "With that, we put together a five-to-seven year plan and decided we would jump back in, really concentrating on the things we weren't as well-versed in to maximize our competitiveness," David explains. "We perfected our rate structure and set forth our guiding priorities, which will always be our customers, our communities, and our employees."

With its foundation deeply rooted in the Christian faith, David and his team strive to infuse their work with the tenets of love, family, integrity, altruism, and charity that so thoroughly permeate the spiritual landscape of 2HB's founders. "As Christian owners, we give a minimum of 10 percent of our profits to a wide array of charities every year," David explains. "As a result, we are proud supporters of everything from churches, to boys and girls clubs, to schools, to scholarship funds, to cancer research. Being able to give back to the community is definitely an intrinsic value of having a business, because seeing the effect that giving has and sharing in that joy is priceless."

Beyond their firm commitment to providing excellent service to their customers, 2HB also sets itself apart through its emphasis on creating a strong sense of family in its company culture. Always adhering to the principle that family comes first, the enterprise offers an unparalleled benefits package that addresses the burdens of its employees on both a macro and micro level, whether it's providing for 100% of the health insurance costs for employees and their families or supplying a monthly grooming allowance that gives the overall package a little something extra.

It is without the shadow of a doubt that David emulates much of this strong emphasis on family from the example set forth by his own father, who worked his way from the bottom to the top at the Social Security Administration over his impressive thirty-year career there. "He worked exceedingly hard, but he never once complained about having to support my sisters and me," David reminisces. "His job was certainly stressful, and yet he never brought his work home with him. When he was home, he was Dad, taking the time to engage me in a whole host of activities that made me a more well-rounded person." Now, with his father embarking on his post-retirement adventures of public speaking and assisting in building a church in Florida, David steps forward to fill his shoes in facing the challenges of balancing work with fatherhood. With a young daughter and son of his own, David recognizes family as the very first of 2HB's core values.

These core values have certainly led the company to success in the seven years since its reopening, having added two principals to its leadership team and 20 employees to its repertoire. David currently works three days per week billable with two days reserved for overhead duties, which are split between business development and office or recruitment matters. This division of labor capitalizes on his extraverted and outgoing nature, which is augmented by a visionary streak that keeps him ever focused on the next big thing. Reginald, an ideal compliment, offers a pragmatic and analytical temper to David's leadership style. "I'm the one who sees a mountain and wants to conquer it, and Reginald is the voice of reason that allows us to consider the proposed course of action from all angles," he explains.

Equipped with this balanced sense of leadership and venerable company culture, 2HB is now poised to assume a projected rate of aggressive growth over the next several years. "Everything we did in 2010 has been gearing up for this," David points out. "People may think we do things backwards, but really it's a methodology oriented around forward thinking and advanced planning. We're way ahead of the curve in terms of our infrastructure and ensuring that our processes are in place, such that we will be equipped to handle the coming growth." In an industry in which a company's capacity to increase revenues is directly regulated by the number of its employees, this preparedness is crucial in ensuring an organic and smooth scaling of the enterprise.

Foresightedness of this magnitude is not honed without experience, and as he advises young entrepreneurs entering the business world today, David emphasizes the importance of seeking a great breadth of knowledge and experience before settling into a given career path. "In a global sense, try to do things that will open up opportunities and ideas that will help shape who you want to be," he urges. "Things are so different outside of the United States, and until you experience that, it's hard to have a nuanced appreciation for where you are, what you have, and who you share this world with. Experience as much as you can while you aren't tied down to a family, career, or job."

Beyond this, David suggests a sincerity of motive and intention in all that one does, as these are sure to shine through to those around you. "As a company, we're going to treat people the way we want to be treated, and we're going to do right by folks," he affirms. "If you give from your heart, people will be able to see that, and it will make all the difference." Pursuing this kind of spirit-filled success leads to the kind of holistic achievement that benefits not only the individual, but also society as a whole, and for this aspect of his character, David credits his parents. "Throughout my life, I have tried to model my career and personal growth after my dad. However, I must credit my mother for the excellent job she did in shaping me as a person," he acknowledges. "I'm blessed to have two wonderful parents that have not only been role models over the course of my life, but two of my best friends as well."

Christos Efessiou

Walking the Wire

When 19-year-old Christos Efessiou left his homeland of Greece to enroll as a senior exchange student at a U.S. high school just west of Boston, it was as though the young man were taking his first bold steps out onto a wire suspended a hundred feet above the ground. He had only one year to learn a language he did not speak and earn admittance to an American college or else he would be forced to return to Greece to work for his father's company—a future that would be undoubtedly secure, yet dishearteningly dependent. Now the founder, President, and CEO of Strategic Pharmaceutical Advisors (SRxA), an international consulting, marketing, and education firm, Christos's story is a testament to every young person's brave first steps out along that quivering, indefinite, yet ultimately rewarding wire of risk.

In an industry in which companies tend to start with a business model and add intellectual assets as projects are acquired, SRxA has devised a stronghold from the supremely unique reverse position of signing on industry leaders and then building a business around that knowledge. "I essentially turned that concept on its head by embracing the idea that, if the equation works from left to right, it should work from right to left as well," Christos explains.

Combining the top Key Opinion Leaders (KOL) in specific clinical fields with the highest expertise in business administration, SRxA has now grown into a force of over 50 independent physicians spread across three continents, 40 of which are campaign leaders and considered to be at the pinnacle of their careers. "These individuals aren't just very good practitioners, but also professors, clinical or otherwise. All conduct research, and they've ascended to the executive offices of their professional colleges, many of which are among the most revered professional academies worldwide," he continues. "I reasoned that, if we could attract such advisors to SRxA, we could capture a good amount of market share, and that's exactly what happened."

SRXA is set up such that the relationships it holds with its opinion leaders are nonexclusive, which actually increases the value of each individual to the firm as a whole. "To me, the greatest value of each person comes from their clinical practice, research, and involvement in their own professional college or academy, which allows them to interact directly with the pharmaceutical industry and remain completely immersed," says Christos. Building the value of each component part of SRxA, then, allows the firm to become so much greater than the sum of its parts, and its clients are well acquainted with this concept. "When someone comes to us for the advice of Dr. X, they know they'll also get the advice of Drs. Y and Z," he explains. "They'll get the opinion of each individual doctor as well as of the collective group, and that is where the value lies."

Today, SRxA is among the only companies that brings together such a compelling sum of top-notch minds in a for-profit environment, and it wields the allure of this status to engender a commitment to steely impartiality, irreproachable ethics, and an unparalleled clarity of thought and advice. "We attain this standard by employing a hard and fast set of rules for our advisors, affirming that SRxA is a corporate entity and that its independent advisors will never be a mouthpiece for anybody," Christos describes. "We always, without fail, deliver a true factual opinion, even if it's not what our clients necessarily want to hear."

And how, exactly, does SRxA's team of gurus ascertain whether a tune is right or not? Information is reverse-engineered to delineate the path to its source. If an error or misrepresentation is found along the way, the path is then re-created going forward, correcting the message that is ultimately generated. It is, at once, a business of integrity and of the highest intellectual prestige, and the repute and expertise engendered through this process are used to provide clean, honest, ethical, and scientifically-based advice to each client.

There is much to be said for such achievements in themselves, but when one takes into account the variables working against Christos and his team, the victories are lent even more sway. "If you operate in pharmaceuticals, you're working in one of the most regulated industries in the country," Christos stresses. "You can do nothing, say nothing, and show nothing unless it has been prescribed by the FDA." Amidst this challenging landscape, much has changed in the past several years that limits the type of work physicians can do, and SRxA has re-engineered its entire concept—not to follow the new regulations, but to stay ahead of them. "If you follow the new regulations, you're a year behind," Christos points out. He is also well-known for staying at the cutting edge of technology, operating the company predominantly wirelessly since it was launched in 2004.

Utilizing these techniques, SRxA grew 100% annually on its advisory side for the first three years, escalating from four advisors to 15. In the three years since, it has added another 20 plus individuals and five new divisions to the company's portfolio. "In a business like this, you're evaluated on both the depth of each specialty and on the breadth across the different clinical specialties that you cover," Christos points out. "Otherwise, you're going to pigeonhole yourself behind certain therapeutic areas which will dictate what market you can follow, and this kind of limitation is just not in the spirit of SRxA."

The structural integrity of his practice, however, is only as successful as the individuals chosen to work within it, and Christos utilizes a leadership style that focuses on knowing who the right people for the job are and then valuing them accordingly. "When I interview, I do so almost exclusively based on the candidate's personality, because you cannot teach someone how to be ethical or personable, or how to work with that kind of bold energy that will give you the rocket boosters you need to get through a demanding project," he says. Once he has brought these people into SRxA, he treats them like the tremendous assets that they are. "My management philosophy has been to tangibly show my team that I value them—possibly more than they value themselves," he adds. "Operating in this mindset inspires people to work ten times as hard and be ten times as loyal."

Christos first came to acquire his keen sense of business while growing up in Greece, where his father—a self-made man—was truly a titan of the durable medical equipment industry. While certainly impressive, his father's footprint left little room for Christos to prime his own impact, which prompted the young man to take the leap and move to America. "Operating on part gut, part intellect, and part self-confidence, I seized the challenge to do what my father himself had done—to see what I was truly capable of," he explains. "I have always been an all-or-nothing person, but never a gambler. I calculate risk fairly well and feel comfortable with probability, knowing that one can't possibly apply himself to the fullest if he knows there's a safety net below. Do your due diligence, go all in, and leap."

The young man had no family in the United States, couldn't speak the language, and had never been away from home before, but he leapt anyway. He picked up English through osmosis and Sesame Street, took the SATs several times, and was admitted to all 36 of the institutions to which he had applied, much to his surprise. "I felt I only knew the language at a rudimentary level, but if a university was willing to take a chance on me, I was willing to be that person," he remembers. His courage was rewarded when he woke up one morning during his freshman year and realized he had dreamed in English the night before. "It was the biggest boost of confidence I had ever known, and nothing could stand in my way after that," he continues, his air captivated by the same exuberance he describes. "My self-assurance went through the roof, and once you feel that, you've got it. From then on it was simply looking at opportunities and capitalizing on them."

Though he began his college career along a premed route, he soon realized that he was far more interested in the business of medicine than the practice of it, and so shifted gears accordingly. When, at the age of 27, Christos found himself degreed, board-certified, and registered in respiratory care, and working in the second highest position available in his specialty, he knew it was time to switch gears once again. With that, on the last day of 1984, he took out a $3,500 loan to pay for a career advisor to help explore his next move. It was this decision that first opened his eyes to the salesperson behind the scientist in his psyche, and several months later, he got the call that would mark the advent of his association with the pharmaceutical industry.

Testing the limits of possibility. This has always been what draws Christos, and what draws others to him. "Anything that had a challenge, I was behind," he remembers. "Anytime anyone said no, it was my license to go do it. If someone said I couldn't do something, I would say, watch me." This willingness to put himself on the line stems from his very compelling definition of the word *failure*.

"There is a big difference between non-success and failure," Christos stresses. "Not succeeding does not necessarily mean you've failed. I believe you fail only when you have firmly decided and convinced yourself that you have, and this is the worst thing you can do to your mindset. I'm not suggesting that you should couch nonsuccesses to make them look like successes, but if you can take the successful elements out of an unsuccessful enterprise, you can always build something from that."

This fundamental belief in the power of the human spirit to create, even in the face of adversity, has been the driving force behind his success. Christos has spent his professional career triumphing over the challenges of a foreign nation and over the myriad intricacies that true entrepreneurship entails. In addition to launching three concurrently operating businesses in the span of a decade and remaining ever ready for the next challenge, Christos has a book in the works that draws a very perceptive line between the art of business and the art of parenting. *CDO: Chief Daddy Officer; The Business of Fatherhood* is slated for release in September of 2011. Promising to be replete with strong values and useful idioms, this book will teach all business professionals and family men the appropriate tools to discover how to use their skills in business to strengthen their families.

"Everything starts with you," Christos reminds us. "Walk your own wire. Stay grounded in reality, but believe that nothing is impossible. If you refuse to let yourself down, you're not going to let other people down either."

Chris Frederick

The Implementation Impetus

"I understand the value of the course, but are your clients actually benefitting from it?"

Chris Frederick paused for a moment, considering his wife's question. As the founder and CEO of Automotive Training Institute (ATI), an organization committed to providing training services to mid-sized automotive repair shops, his primary concern had always been the training programs themselves and not so much their aftermath. Every satisfaction survey he had administered indicated that his clients loved the one-week management training sessions ATI had recently launched, and that was good enough for him.

"Is their business improving in the long term? If you visited them a year later, is your impact visible? Have you really changed their lives?" she pressed.

"Isn't that beyond the scope of what we do?" he responded.

The answer to that question was *yes*, but in that moment, Chris's perspective transformed. Sure, it was the accurate answer, but was it the *right* answer? Was ATI truly changing the lives of the shop owners who had come to the organization in the hopes of turning their businesses around and taking them to the next level?

Interested in exploring his wife's query about the effectiveness of his training programs, he decided to administer a new kind of survey—one that would measure the long-term impact of the information imparted. The results were startling. Only about one in a hundred participants had actually implemented the recommendations put forth by the training programs, and as a result, very few had actually seen tangible gains.

"I've always had a passion for making people successful," Chris remarks now, "so I found this extremely disheartening." With that, he decided to hire a coach to follow up with participants post-program to promote actual change. "It made a huge difference, and the shop owners were actually going home and implementing the knowledge and education they had paid a good deal of money for," he reports. "Coaching is so much more important than training, and it was around this time—in the nineties—that we realized we're really a coaching program."

ATI was first launched in 1974 and originally focused on technician training, with a shift into management training in 1985 when they started selling accounting software and point of sale systems, assisting shops in the automating process. The subsequent transition into seminars and training programs led the way for the final evolution into coaching but was originally pursued in an effort to sell more equipment, not necessarily to help people. The business model was excellent, and the training programs sold out regionally three months in advance. Chris's motivation to pursue coaching, then, was certainly not for lack of success.

After the initial plunge into coaching, ATI took on 18 coaches in under ten years as the business continued to double at an unprecedented growth rate. Chris and his team penetrated North America, opening a call center that spoke to 10,000 of the country's 150,000 shops monthly and was extremely effective in accessing those individuals who were truly committed to learning and growing their businesses.

Today, ATI has perfected its model and stands at the forefront of its industry. Its target niche is automotive repair shop owners that generate between $400 thousand and $6 million in revenues annually, with the majority of their clients being little ma-and-pa, family-owned businesses with a handful of corporate clients tossed in the mix. Though the price tag on their training and coaching program is certainly an investment at $45 thousand, many would argue that it's worth every penny. Shop owners get 30 months of intensive and personalized attention focused at improving their business, with the initial focus aimed at fixing cash flow and addressing other financial aspects.

Once the business becomes profitable again, Chris and his team focus in installing systems to help it run consistently. This is accomplished through addressing customer interaction, whether it's customer service or sales skills. The second half of the program, then, concentrates on developing leadership skills in either the principal of the company or the second in command in preparation for the leader's retirement.

"Most of our clients are baby boomers who started off very small and working over a hundred hours per week doing everything for themselves," Chris explains. "They burn themselves out, and their families get upset because they're never home. We get them to the next stage making more money and working only 40 or 50 hours a week, and I can't tell you the number of times I've had wives come up to me and thank me for giving them their husbands back and turning their family business around. Those are some of the best moments."

What truly makes ATI unique is the fact that it backs its product with a promise of financial accountability that actually guarantees success. While there are a number of competitors out there who offer a course here or a course there with no tangible pledge or follow up, Chris and his team offer a two-to-one guarantee, with an average of $80 to $90 thousand in gains in the first year or 30 months to double their clients' investments. "Our guarantee makes us more accountable because we're actually invested in the success of our clients, just as our clients are invested in us," Chris points out. "That, plus the fact that we're a complete solution and not a little a la cart band-aid to a short-term problem, gets us those clients who are long-term thinkers and truly committed to turning their businesses around."

Since the implementation of the coaching program, ATI has grown to 80 employees, with 50 concentrated in the D.C. metro area and another 30 spread across North America. After averaging $1 million in annual revenue in the nineties, it now boasts a strong $12 million and has largely managed to dodge the bullet of the recession, maintaining their client base through the trying times of late.

Much of Chris's success draws from the fact that he has dedicated his professional career to his lifelong passion, refusing to deny his inner pull despite the urgings of others. Indeed, his father had loved cars, and thus he grew up amongst revered 57 Thunderbirds, beloved Lincolns, and other high-end sports cars that inspired in him a similar devotion. He enrolled in the University of Maryland for college but was academically dismissed midway through his freshman year because street racing had consumed a considerable amount of his time and resources. "I was more interested in going to the state park and waxing my family's Corvette than going to class," Chris remembers.

After his father forced him to sell the Corvette and return to school, he acquired the 427 Camaro that would steal his heart yet again. "It was what they call a sleeper," he laughs now. "It had dog dish hub caps and no markings, but a big motor straight from the factory." Street racing took center stage in his life yet again, and he was making $500 a week. Still, he invested himself in the college courses that were of true value to him and excelled at his sales, public speaking, and business classes. After several years, though, he felt he had learned everything he needed from academia and discussed his situation with his father.

"You should be doing something you're passionate about," his father had said. "Don't worry about making money just yet." With that encouragement, Chris found a straight-commission position selling engine analyzers, which he embraced wholeheartedly. After several years there, however, he found himself disagreeing with the integrity of the company and felt as though he could run things better himself. Thus, at the age of 24, he parted ways with the company with four other salespeople following in his wake, and in 1974, ATI was born. "It was my first company and I had no idea what I was doing," Chris recalls. "I just knew I could do better in representing the interests of shop owners."

As ATI continued Chris's legacy of selling engine analyzers, it became clear that his people skills would serve him well in years to come. "I came into the business world at a young age and with the ability to motivate other people to act," he observes now. "I can figure out what people want, and I can help them get it. Through my communication and sales skills, I was able to sell people on a concept, and this was pivotal in shaping the company and its future success."

The most fascinating thing about Chris's skill set, however, is that it is just as cultivated as it is innate. "I'm definitely an introvert, and I didn't like speaking or being in front of people," he remarks of his childhood. "I didn't like networking or social situations in which there were a lot of people." It wasn't until he tackled his public speaking class in college that he was able to overcome this obstacle that stood in the way of what he hoped to accomplish in life, and his success in doing so is truly remarkable. "I realized that I had this immense desire to accomplish a lot in life and that I was going to have to do things I wasn't crazy about in order to do so," he adds. "I really did fake it until I made it."

Especially in his earlier years, Chris would literally turn himself on every morning and then off again every afternoon at five o'clock, much to the confusion of friends and family who were privy to both versions of him. "At some point, you really assimilate this new version of you into yourself and it ceases to be an effort," he explains. "I became more comfortable with it, and I saw that I was helping people, and this really helped motivate me to get out there and push the limits of my comfort zone the way I did."

In advising young entrepreneurs entering the workforce today, Chris cautions against emulating his own decision to skip out early on his education. "Stay in school," he urges. "Even though you may read about people who become extremely successful without finishing, the odds are not good. Get your education and supplement it through interning or experimenting in businesses you have a passion for." Broadening this suggestion, he details the importance of weighing the long-term outcome of any decision. Embrace those choices that expand your options, and steer away from those that will impose limitations upon you. "Try not to let yourself get tied down," he says. "It's a terrible thing for young people to get boxed in and stop taking risks."

In following the example of his own professional advice and actively pursuing change through implementation, Chris is now looking toward the future as he frees up more of his own time to focus on growing ATI. It is clear, however, that this drive stems from the opportunity to transform rather than the opportunity for self gain. "When we were regionalized, we had an impact on four or five hundred shop owners," he explains. "Now we impact around twenty thousand between our one-day seminars and our coaching program. My father always said that the more people you help, the more you'll grow, the more money you'll make, and the more impact you'll be able to have. In envisioning the future of ATI, it is with this principle in mind that we press forward."

Richard Gargagliano

The Inspiration of the Inspired

It is often argued that a rational approach to life is far more logical than the act of relying upon gut instinct. Research suggests, however, that the intuitive sense imparted through such instincts may offer a more thorough, comprehensive, and instantaneous catalogue of logic than any labored practice in rational exploration could hope to impart. For Richard Gargaliano, it was precisely this inner sense of intuition that led him down a serendipitous path toward professional success and personal fulfillment that he could never have found without the courage to pursue the urging of a hunch.

Richard first sensed the whisper of this hunch when he attended a showing of the film *Black Stallion*, a stirring portrayal of the life of a horse. Having never ridden a horse in his life, Richard wasn't quite sure why he found the film so enthralling, but he felt compelled to see it in theaters a second and third time. "I can't quite place my finger on it, but I think I was inspired by the notion of trying to do something impossible," Richard remembers. "The notion of doing something that completely defied the boundaries of what people consider to be possible really touched me, and the horse became the icon that brought this whole concept together for me."

Seeking fuel to keep the dream alive, Richard enrolled in horseback riding lessons and took a course at the University of Maryland on caring for horses. "I didn't know what I was going to do with it all; it was as if I was just collecting fuel for the dream until the right path became clear to me." This moment arrived one unassuming day when, sitting at home, he came across an Help Wanted advertisement calling for a horse hospital administrator. With a textured background in hospital administration, Richard felt as though fate were almost palpable. "I knew it was my ticket… My gateway into what I was supposed to be doing," he reports. Now the COO for the Marion DuPont Scott Equine Medical Center in Leesburg, Virginia, the rest is history.

To truly grasp the unique angles of the story, one must dive a little deeper into this history. Richard's eventual involvement in the medical field first took root when he found himself interested in sports and health while playing football at the University of Massachusetts. When his interest in a vocation as a football coach evolved into an interest in medicine, he wanted to be a doctor but didn't have a fitting academic record. When an advisor remarked that he would make a great hospital administrator, however, his interest was immediately piqued. Graduating in 1973 with a BS in public health, he then earned a master's in the same field at the University of North Carolina.

"I finished that, and all I wanted was to save the world," he recalls. He believed he had found an opportunity to do just that when he accepted his first job with the United Mine Workers Health and Retirement Fund, which stationed Richard and his new bride in the remote and backwoods setting of Logan, West Virginia. It was a rough place, but the couple set to work right away, with his wife Joan working at a local health center and Richard recruiting doctors to help improve the lives of coal miners and their families.

"I soon realized, however, that the fairy tale wasn't what it seemed, as the industry was fraught with corruption," he explains, indicating that his reaction to *Black Stallion* may not have been the first time gut instinct came in handy. "As I gained more practical work experience and developed a keener eye for what was going on, I became a witness for a Federal government investigation and was able to assist with cleaning up the enterprise." Richard was then moved to Washington, DC, to provide assistance with the development of surveillance systems aimed to ensure that such programs were administered correctly.

From there, he accepted a position with Howard University Hospital, where his sense of professional accomplishment was forever altered by the influence of a supervisor who took a vested interest in his potential. "It was the first time I had had a mentor who really believed in me, and it was truly empowering," Richard describes. "It was among the most important things I've gotten out of a job, as it imparted a new sense of self-confidence."

It was perhaps this element of self-confidence that won Richard the position at the Equine Medical Center, as the experience of applying for the vacancy acquired a sort of self-actualizing air. "I was convinced before I even went to the interview that I had the job," he remembers. "I felt so powerful, equipped with this sense of fulfillment and destiny." Indeed, it was as if he had been preparing for this opportunity for years, honing his skills as a successful healthcare services administrator yet unsure of which health sector he hoped to apply those skills to. With his intuitive draw toward the notion of conquering the impossible as portrayed in *Black Stallion*, it was almost as if the horse were the symbol that brought the threads of his life full-circle.

"I don't think there are many people who could approach this job with the same level of passion as I do," Richard remarks. "I envisioned myself in that position in my mind, and I think this showed in the interview." He didn't leave his destiny up to chance alone, however. Noting that most candidates would probably shake the hands of the various department heads and send them a written follow-up letter, he took it upon himself to sit down for an extended period of time with each department head after his two-hour interview. "Reasoning that I had nothing to lose, I went around to everyone," he remembers. "When you really feel that you're an extraordinary fit for a position, exhibiting a standard level of interest just won't cut it."

Richard's dogged determination paid off, but winning the position was only the beginning of the challenging yet rewarding career path that has led him to where he is today. The Equine Medical Center, which is part of Virginia Tech's Regional College of Veterinary Medicine, serves to train veterinarians of the future in medicine and surgery. Its 150-person hospital offers advanced healthcare services to the roughly 200,000 horses that populate the Mid-Atlantic 4-state area, approximately 3,000 of which frequent the hospital per year.

The hospital was first conceived of in 1983, when Marion duPont Scott wished to give a legacy gift of $4 million to Virginia Tech to sponsor a hospital that would address the need for regional emergency services for horses. 200 acres of land were donated to the cause, and as Virginia Tech had intended to start a specialty teaching hospital for horses, it entering the mix as well. The building was constructed and opened for business in 1984, and today, the hospital is funded through a public-private partnership, with a heavy emphasis on the private.

When Richard took the helm in 1987, his belief in triumphing over seemingly impossible tasks would be put to the test from the outset. Having operated on a deficit since its inception, the hospital was heavily in debt, yet Richard was not discouraged. "I was so excited about the job that these typical red flags were not red flags to me at all," he explains. This unwavering sense of commitment undoubtedly stems from the deep inner connection he feels for his vocation, which lends him the fervor to weather any storm. "This hospital is a destination for people to achieve their dreams," he affirms. "It changes lives and saves lives. When people entrust us to save their animals, which are so often a symbol of sacrifice and love for their families, it is an honor and a privilege to have the opportunity to do that, and we don't take it lightly." From this conviction, Richard has fashioned a future for the hospital that few would have thought possible when he first started with the organization.

How, exactly, has he accomplished such a feat? "As people, we tend to live too much day-to-day," Richard points out, "but unless the day-to-day is framed in the context of the past and the future, it becomes meaningless. If you don't have the vantage points of where you've come from and where you're going, where we are right now is rendered meaningless. For example, our fundraising projections indicate that, by the year 2050, two-thirds of the hospital will be funded by donors alone, which means it is very possible that, someday, any horse will be able to seek treatment here regardless of their owner's ability to pay."

Richard's methodology for keeping the hospital enterprise moving forward, then, is to use the power inherent in this vision of the future to prevent today from being an excuse for failure. "When you put that vision out in front of constituents, they're willing to help you with today's problem because they know you have a future," he points out. Applying this mindset to academics, personal life, or whatever entity one believes in inspires a confidence that enables one to see today's problems as miniscule and tomorrow's triumphs as imminent.

Richard's vision is nothing short of inspired, and it is precisely in this uplifting worldview that his story and leadership style instill inspiration in others. "I always thought of myself as being inspired, not inspirational, but then I realized that there isn't really a difference between the two," he reflects. "If you're inspired by the forces that affect you, then you also have the opportunity to be inspirational to others, and it is in this capacity that you can compel people to believe that anything can happen."

In advising young entrepreneurs embarking on their professional careers today, Richard stresses the importance of finding a vocation that inspires true passion in the individual, for that investment of heart and soul enables one to rise above whatever challenge they might confront. "Take enough time to figure out what's most important in your life and then go for it," he urges. "When you're lucky enough to find what you love to do and then follow it, you won't go home troubled at night wondering what you're supposed to be or wondering if you've failed, and that's a wonderful feeling. When we discover what we're meant to be and follow it, it's like a self-sustaining fire." It is this fire that burns the impossible into the possible, at once inspirational and inspired.

Suresh Gursahaney

The Self-Directed Solution

Twenty minutes of American music. As a young boy spending the summer with his grandparents in India during monsoon season, Suresh Gursahaney yearned for the singular joy imparted by such an interlude, and he was going to do something about it. His maternal grandfather was co-owner of Bush Radio, the second largest electronic radio manufacturer in India, and Suresh would follow him to work each day, enamored with the art of business ownership as much as with the art of electronics. He learned much about both as he sat beside his grandfather and built an AM radio, which he took home that night and hooked up to the big antenna outside of their apartment building. Each night thereafter, at three in the morning, he would wake up to tune in to WABC out of New York for those twenty blessed minutes—twenty minutes of American music.

"That's how I got into electronics," Suresh remarks. Now the President and CEO of MicroAutomation Incorporated of Virginia, Suresh's story has followed a unique path that has successfully synthesized family expectations with individual calling.

Suresh's father had come to America to attend Purdue University before returning to India to start a family through a traditional arranged marriage. He and his new wife then returned to America for a fresh start, where he worked for GE. As the patriarch of the family, Mr. Gursahaney took it upon himself to bring his parents and each of his eight siblings over from India, one by one. This made for an exceptionally enriching childhood for Suresh, who was the first Indian born in Louiseville, Kentucky. "I had the opportunity to live with each of my cousins for six months at a time, and my paternal grandfather was the one to always check my homework and help me learn math," Suresh remembers. "As a result, my extended family has an incredible bond."

Mr. Gursahaney believed firmly that his children should earn whatever they received, so Suresh learned the value of hard work at an early age. At 12, he picked up a paper route around the neighborhood, and he hasn't stopped working for more than two weeks at a time since that day. In college, he would work during holidays as a dishwasher or at McDonalds, until he got a job working the nightshift at a computer company. "I learned programming in my spare time in the middle of the night as I monitored jobs running on the mainframe," he recalls. "By the end of the summer, I had written a blackjack program."

His family had always expected him to pursue a career as either a doctor or a lawyer, but Suresh felt an insatiable draw toward the technological realm in which he had dabbled. One of his uncles worked for IBM at the time, and a family gathering over Christmas of his senior year of college at Duke University presented the perfect opportunity to introduce his own interest in such a career path.

"Don't bother applying," his uncle had said discouragingly. "Your GPA is a 3.25, and they won't even consider anything under a 3.75."

Knowing that his computer science and engineering coursework GPA was actually a 3.9, Suresh heard these words not as a ultimatum, but instead as a challenge, resolving to apply to each and every IBM location in the United States. When he hadn't heard anything by March, he was about to contact his previous place of employment when he suddenly received the call that would forever alter the course of his future. That summer, he was given a three-month contract with IBM's Federal systems division, and that one chance was all he needed.

Fresh out of college and ecstatic at the opportunity to pursue his dream, Suresh hit the ground running at IBM and soon noticed that his work ethic far exceeded the pace of the corporate culture that surrounded him. Remaining impervious to the influence of his surroundings, he maintained his dogged commitment to his work until the summer ended and he was called into his boss's office. "You know, there were a couple months there that you were the only one contributing to this organization," his supervisor told him, supplementing the compliment with an offer of full-time employment.

Suresh had promised his father and grandfather that he would get his MBA promptly out of college, but IBM wouldn't take no for an answer, so he made a deal with Mr. Gursahaney that he would attend business school two years later in order to take advantage of this immediate opportunity. "Once you start working, you'll never want to go back to school," his father had said, but he reluctantly agreed.

Within two years, Suresh was already running a full project at IBM, but true to his word, he was admitted to the MBA program at Carnegie Melon. His supervisor, however, pleaded with him to defer his plans one more year, which Suresh agreed to do. The following year, he was granted an educational leave of absence to fulfill his promise to his family, after which he resumed his position at IBM for another four years. The company was in its heyday at the time, but Suresh sensed whispers of mortality in the framework indicating a mentality that wouldn't survive in the marketplace for much longer. "They seemed to believe that customers would buy the software just because it was developed by IBM, or that their products would dictate the market instead of vice versa," he remembers.

Working for the applications solutions division at the time, Suresh was spearheading a project to automate the call centers and reduce costs using computer telephony integration for Northeast Utilities. Gauging market demand and figuring that the resulting piece of software could be developed as a more universal product instead of an individual solution, he approached management with the idea but was promptly turned down on the grounds that their division didn't handle such matters. Undeterred as per his usual, Suresh then enlisted Northeast Utilities itself to tout the idea, which IBM then embraced with open arms.

Though pleased that the software would be shrink-wrapped and sold, Suresh's faith in the company as a whole was waning, and he seized the opportunity to strike out on his own in 1991. His vision was to launch a company that would serve as the middleman between IBM and the customer base, offering the kind of innovative and solutions-oriented service that he believed in. "Customers were moving into a mode of wanting to buy a solution, not a product," he explains. "There was a gap between the product put out by IBM and the solution customers were looking for, and we arose to fill that void." With that, MicroAutomation was born.

MicroAutomation serves the technology and automation needs of call centers through a wide range of services, whether it be reporting, interactive voice response systems, or tools that make agents more productive. Since its inception 20 years ago, Suresh has migrated beyond the bounds of IBM products to adapt a more vendor-agnostic approach that allows them to readily adapt to the environments of their clientele. "We're a system integration firm rather than a product firm," he points out.

Suresh's father, brother and sister all pursued and maintained professional journeys through the corporate, big company realm, so Suresh's decision to veer off the beaten path and pursue a small business experience was met with much initial dismay. "I didn't have much support," he concedes, "but this only made me work harder."

During its first twelve years, MicroAutomation was content to establish itself as a small yet reliable firm of just under a dozen employees with revenues of about $1.7 million annually. "I had very little opportunity to engage in strategic or tactical thinking because I was so immersed in the day to day processes of keeping the organization running," Suresh reflects. "Essentially, I was the sole decision maker, and all the projects ran through me. I soon found, though, that running the company at that size took too great a personal toll, and it was time to grow so that we could get a management team firmly in place."

To instigate the growth he envisioned, Suresh first assembled an advisory board and then supplemented this input by joining a CEO coaching organization called Vistage, which proved invaluable to his future endeavors. "The program exposed me to a number of CEOs that, surprisingly, were facing many of the same challenges I was," he says. "I then made it my personal goal to grow the company to a point where I could extricate myself from daily operations and shifting my focus back on what I left IBM to do in the first place, which is architecting solutions."

Since that resolution took effect, MicroAutomation underwent a steep growth curve and now employs a team of over thirty individuals, with revenues clocking in at slightly over $8 million. "Establishing a management team is exceptionally arduous in that each individual has to really know the business before you release the reigns," Suresh points out. "You have to feel comfortable that that person is committed to the business and will fulfill your vision of where the company needs to go. Still, we have finally reached that point, which allows me to really immerse myself in what I love to do—strategies and solutions."

It is with this commitment to his passions fresh in mind that Suresh offers several guiding principles to young entrepreneurs entering the business world today. "Whatever you're going to do, do it for the right reasons," he stresses. "Don't take a job just because it's the first one that comes along or because it happens to have a bigger paycheck. Do something you love. You'll enjoy your life more while also being more dedicated to your work, and as your expertise develops, so will the monetary rewards."

Suresh pairs this idiom with a healthy dose of forward thinking, which can always be reinforced by the influence of a mentor. "Plan for the future now and don't wait to begin saving for retirement," he says. "Make choices that will pay off in the long run, even if they boast less short-term glamour." For anyone pursuing a self-directed solution, adhering to such principles promises a path that is not only successful, but in line with the inner drive through which we might achieve our highest potential.

Lillian I. Harris

Growing the Family

In early 1990, Calvin B. Harris, a retired senior chief with a PhD in psychology, set a dream in motion. Cal had finished his career in the Navy a decade earlier, and after ten years of consulting for government contracting firms in fields related to human factors engineering and industrial psychology, he was determined to start his own business. He wanted a business that would grow to become a family, where no employee was merely a number, where friends would work together to perform at their best. With this vision in mind, on January 24, he founded Man-Machine Systems Assessment. And from the start, his daughter Lillian and wife Martha were closely involved.

While she may have started out making photocopies and hanging out in the office while doing her school work, Lilly Harris is now the President and CEO of MSA. And though she says that she was "just a kid" at the time, it quickly becomes apparent that she was paying very close attention. "My father always referred to our employees as our MSA family," she says, "and he was always trying to grow that family." Now, even though it's 21 years later and he no longer directly oversees the company, her father's legacy is still alive and well as MSA strives to promote a sense of family and connection throughout its team of employees. No one is a number. Everyone is a name.

According to Lilly, her father was something of a serial entrepreneur over the years following his departure from the military. Even so, she reveals that, at the time he founded MSA, he still had much to learn when it came to business. His strength lay in taking a visionary idea and starting a company, but not necessarily in running the enterprise that resulted. In fact, while he was founding MSA, he was also starting a business manufacturing bicycle grips.

"Even as a kid, my father was always involved in business," Lilly reports. "He had a paper route before the age of ten. He fought forest fires, and in high school he ran the ticket club at school." Like her father, Lilly has been a natural entrepreneur from early childhood. But where her father had had his paper route, Lilly was delighted to set up a lemonade stand, organize a garage sale, or sell baked goods and coffee. "We would bake the muffins, brew the coffee, and I would price out the items," she reminisces. "Muffins were fifty cents, coffee a quarter." Lilly would also price items in the garage sales, going so far as to negotiate with customers any item's worth with aplomb.

She was also very competitive in activities like school fundraisers. She enjoyed forming relationships with her neighbors, never too shy to call on them when she had a new cause. By the time she was age 13, the whole neighborhood knew her very well. "They would know it was that time of year again," she says. "If I was selling chocolate for the soccer team, I was determined to sell the most chocolate." In fact, her competitive nature regularly earned her the honor of top fundraiser in junior high and high school.

Lilly would even negotiate contracts with her parents over pet ownership and its many responsibilities. Along with her father, she would take out a paper napkin at a diner and map all the items out, then type up a contract that would be subject to another round of negotiating before approval. "In sum," Lilly says, "negotiating to create value came very naturally to me."

Planning things out on a napkin was a custom they carried long into her adulthood, and it served them well much later as Lilly found herself at a crossroads, considering whether to go all-in with MSA or to exit and pursue one of her alternate plans that she refers to now as her "Plan Bs", including becoming a chef, joining the peace corps to travel the world, or becoming a film producer. She was in her early twenties at the time, having already attained her bachelor's degree and left Texas to work at MSA's D.C. office for about two years. For those two years she had been in "hard-core learning mode" and was paired up with a retired Army Colonel whom Lilly refers to as "Dutch" and who proved a very important mentor figure in her life. She saw many ways that she thought she could improve the company and sophisticate it, but she struggled with being the boss's daughter and had a hard time evolving her role. "I think I've always been a visionary-type," Lilly says, "someone who sees the big picture and thinks just as big." After two years at MSA she felt like a small piece in a large puzzle and couldn't figure out how to fit. She wasn't sure she wanted to stay.

Lilly describes a scene at a diner table one day as a moment where her father saw that she was frustrated and unhappy. "He'd always been the dreamer," she says, "the guy who says, 'As long as you're happy, I'm happy.'" They took out a placemat and wrote down all the many things she liked to do. "I love movies, I love music, I'm an artist—it's in my spirit," she recounts. Lilly found government contracts to be very dry and somewhat corporate for her taste, feeling as though she couldn't truly express herself in such a venue at that point. How could she unite her many artistic inclinations with her business skills to provide a streamlined, unique, and compelling service? "Together," she says, "we came up with the idea that I could go into producing movies. The film industry."

Lilly attended an intensive program at NYU Film School and worked twelve- to fifteen-hour days learning the ins and outs of script writing, film production, and the business side of film. She ended up producing two short films, feeling at last that she was in her element. Her parents were convinced she wasn't coming back to MSA. But as it turned out, it was her experience producing these short films that enabled her to return to MSA and affect a profound shift in her role to one that would allow her to fully express her visionary nature.

"One kid working on one of our film projects had $1,200 that his dad had given us," Lilly explains. "We had a full budget to write a project management timeline, take care of the logistics, and achieve the creative vision we had in mind. There were so many moving parts." Lilly was the executive producer of the project, and suddenly, everything started to click. It was a business process from start to finish, and the exhilaration she hadn't felt when she started at MSA was now shining through the seams of her character. She had only felt like a small piece of the company before, but when she came back to MSA shortly after the film program ended in 2006 to help stabilize its accounting department, she was at once fired up and loving it.

"Everything finally worked," she gushes. "I just said to myself, 'OK, this is a movie. This is MSA's movie.'" Lilly needed a business plan, a crew, a budget, and a vision for the end product. Once she began to conceptualize of MSA in this way, her innate creativity was no longer boxed out by the business world, but rather became its lifeblood. "All I needed to do was remain interested and passionate, and I had found the framework for that," Lilly explains. "And that's how I've been running MSA ever since."

Before she would become president and eventually CEO however, Lilly worked under the previous President of MSA, who began as a mentor to her but eventually became a peer. "He treated me more like a daughter," Lilly laughs. "After struggling to be the boss's daughter in my first stretch with MSA, it now seemed like I was the President's daughter. He worked hard to get me to think more strategically, teaching me about the government contracting industry and helping to lay the foundation for what has now become my career. Ultimately, he would leave the company to pursue his Ph.D. "His departure posed a big challenge for me," Lilly remembers. "I wasn't sure I was ready for the challenge to take on a larger role in the company."

Lilly reports now that she was scared at the time, as MSA was in debt. "I don't know how I did it, but within a year we were out of debt and had started growing again," she reports. Since then she has overseen a sweeping re-branding campaign and has refined and diversified the company from the core technical niche in a way that her father never could have imagined.

Now that MSA is out of the woods and flourishing, Lilly credits her strong support system for her endurance over the years, whether it was hours-long telephone conversations or just having friends stand and applaud as MSA began to win industry awards. "Every little victory," she says, "every employee we added, turning that red into black, my family and friends were there to encourage me and celebrate the small victories. They're happy for me."

In reflecting back on her journey and its eventual success, Lilly credits most of all her strong relationships and her curiosity about life and business. She implores young people to never stop learning and diversifying themselves, as professional progress is tied strongly to personal momentum and vise versa. "Diversity makes you interesting and a well-rounded human being," she says. Also of vital importance is to find a way to be unique in the workplace. Returning to Texas Tech recently to address students there, she emphasized the importance of relationships and networking. "A relationship requires nurturing. It's a living thing, and without care, it can die," she explains. "Find unique ways to constantly improve yourself and deepen your connections with the people around you."

With so much success already in her wake, what is Lilly's goal moving forward? MSA currently has 55 employees, and just as her father did, Lilly would like to grow that family. By how much?

"Five hundred," she says with a smile.

Kris Hart

The Transformative Power of Human Capital

11—the number of banks 22-year-old Kris Hart had to interview with before he was granted the loan that would begin translating his business dreams into reality. 36—the number of retail locations the young entrepreneur had to inspect before he found the ideal venue in the Foggy Bottom region of Washington, D.C. Now the founder and CEO of Hart Strategic Enterprises, Kris's journey is accented with a dogged determination and creative coping style that refused to take no for an answer.

"Everyone turned me down because I was so young, with no money and no experience," he remembers. "It took a year from the day I began developing the business plan to the day we opened our doors. Even after the loan and the location were taken care of, we still had to secure two investors and lease all the equipment." When the fledgling tanning salon opened for business on March 3, 2006, the end of one journey marked the beginning of a long and thrilling road to come.

Founded in 2005, Hart Strategic Enterprises is a parent company that serves as an engine for small business development and growth. First initiated as one small company with the advent of the tanning salon, the enterprise now manages three businesses and looks for niche opportunities to continue its growth and diversification into virtually any sector. "It's essentially a breeding ground to bring together different individuals who might have ideas so they can find innovative ways to fill a void in any kind of market," Kris explains.

Kris grew up in Bluebell, Pennsylvania, just north of Philadelphia. His father was a courier for Fedex for 35 years, and his mother raised Kris and his three siblings while trying to start her own business. His parents divorced when he was nine years old, and as a result, he transferred schools five times between fifth and tenth grade. It was around this time that the young man first developed an interest in politics, and one night in 1998 while working at a local tavern trying to save up money to buy a car, Congressman John Fox happened to waltz through the door.

With the encouragement of his father, young Kris marched right up to the Representative to ask questions about how he came into his position and, fascinated by the boy's boldness, Fox asked Kris if he'd like to sit down. Kris declined, saying that he had to work, but when his boss nodded that it was okay, he accepted. Fox then invited him to come onboard as an intern in his office the next day and later told him about the Page Program in Washington, D.C. Though Fox lost the election that year, Kris still applied with the program and moved to Washington soon thereafter.

Later, when Kris was a junior at George Washington University, he served as student body president and, as a result, took a lighter course load so he could focus on his political ambitions. During his senior year, however, he realized that the unique stress and strain of politics wasn't what he wanted after all. "Through my extracurricular activities on campus and throughout the community, I realized that I enjoyed leading a team with a particular vision in mind, exploring innovative concepts as we progress toward a given goal," he reflects. "I knew there must be some way to pursue this passion outside the political realm."

Realizing that going private would allow him to lead in this manner, he decided to take the tremendous risk of leaving college before graduation to focus entirely on the development of his own ideas and business concepts. "I knew I needed to take my own approach," he remembers. "I knew I'd rather write a business plan, marketing strategy, and competition analysis for my own business rather than working on someone else's."

And with that, Kris commenced authoring 19 business proposals. "I love the innovation and art of writing proposals from start to finish," he gushes. "It's like writing the story of a business, complete with imagining the characters that will be needed to tell it."

The bulk of these proposals, however, were for companies that required over a million dollars in startup costs, as well as expertise and experience. Determining that he needed to start small with a fairly straightforward business model in order to build capital and repute, he used the internet to research the prospect of opening the tanning salon. He went in 50/50 with a business partner, and neither took a salary for the first year of operation. Instead, Kris worked from nine to three at the salon and took a restaurant job at night, while his partner worked a catering job in the mornings and covered the salon from three to nine at night. With the incessantly long hours and the help of three employees, the business was doing well after its first year, and the two partners were able to keep their loans current with funds to spare, paying off the bulk of the debt within the first three years of operation.

After hiring more employees for the salon, Kris began to consider his next step. "The next logical transition was something that could serve as a tangential business where we could offer our clients more services," he says. Thus, he decided to wield their tremendous location with easy access to George Washington University and downtown D.C., aiming to open a nearby retail location with a full-service spa that would offer manicures, pedicures, UV and spray tanning, facials, waxing, and massages at one location. "It's sort of like the Wal-Mart mentality of doing everything across the board in one place," he explains. "It truly takes into consideration the needs of our clientele and what we could offer that would make their lives easier."

When it became clear that Kris and his partner did not see eye to eye on how to proceed, Kris bought him out. Almost immediately, he negotiated a contract to take on a second retail location, and Relax Spa was born eight weeks later. After a year of learning the art of running a spa, Kris was then approached by a woman who offered to sell him Foggy Bottom Grocery, which had been a staple of the area since it opened in 1946.

"It's a constant learning curve," Kris explains, referring to the range of sectors held under the ever-expanding umbrella of his company. "With each business adding diversification to our portfolio and escalating in size, the idea was that we were leveraging our revenues to buy bigger businesses." Now, with the addition of a sandwich shop to the grocery store, Kris's portfolio not only extends into the food business, but also exhibits particular emphasis on quality control. The breadth of these industry sectors, as well, lends more credit in the eyes of future investors. "Our background demonstrates that our business proposals and capabilities are solid in themselves, even if we don't have prior experience in a given industry," Kris says. "Our history indicates that, even without direct experience, our method is translatable and still holds the key to success."

So how, exactly, does Hart Strategic Enterprises determine when to launch its next strategic enterprise? Kris approaches such matters through the utilization of a logical formula that helps him in assessing that perfect moment. "I use our three operating businesses as a barometer of how we're doing financially, operationally, and logistically," he explains. "Once these indicators match a certain criteria and pass the appropriate litmus test, I'll begin examining the proposals we have on the backburner to decide which to pull the trigger on."

When this moment comes, Kris forecasts that the next business on the company's agenda will be aligned with the bigger concepts that Hart Strategic Enterprises was originally built to pursue. Such innovative pursuits, however, entail a level of risk that most people find discouraging, and Kris readily acknowledges the potential hazards. "When you come up with an idea that nobody's done before, it's either because it's so innovative that no one has thought of it yet, or that nobody's accomplished it because it doesn't work," he explains. "Most often, it's the latter." In order to steer clear of this, Kris draws from a wide range of resources to build a perspective that is maximally informed and, therefore, maximally effective. "My favorite part of my job is reading newspapers and magazines, studying the market, studying other countries, and staying informed about what people are doing," he reflects.

Kris also bounces ideas off what he refers to as the company's "Strategy Team"—a group of six to eight individuals hand-picked for their innovative thinking and groundbreaking perspectives. The Strategy Team meets every other Wednesday night to discuss business problems, questions, strategy, and analysis. "My ultimate goal is not to be the head of some multibillion dollar company, but only that we develop the kind of financial and professional leverage to really tackle new challenges, to have the leeway to really run with things, and to grow the company the way we want to grow it," he reports.

Looking back at his journey thus far, Kris reflects that the best decision he's made has been the people he surrounds himself with. "I'm good at identifying my own strengths and weaknesses and then pulling in the right people to complement them and to help run the business," he remarks. "I'm always making mental lists of the types of people who would be great to partner with, both now and in the future. Human capital is the greatest resource my company will ever have because it's these people that will come up with innovative ideas and strategies, ultimately determining the company's success."

Kris not only recognizes the importance of human capital in maintaining his company, but also emphasizes the prominent role it has played in bringing him to where he is today. Being a student at George Washington University, for example, enabled him to form so many of the connections that have ultimately shaped Hart Strategic Enterprises. "I met all five of our investors while I was an undergrad, as well as people who have become my landlords, my lawyers, or contacts I know in the Chamber of Commerce," Kris points out. "The actual college classes were certainly helpful, but the networking afforded to me through my undergrad experience is what really made the difference." Thus, in advising young entrepreneurs entering the business world today, he highlights the importance of seizing every opportunity available. "Go out, meet as many different people as you can, get involved in a variety of situations, and learn how things work from the inside out," he says.

Not only is human capital the means for Kris, but also the end goal, the end legacy, and the end source of pride. Indeed, throughout the immensely rewarding experience of translating a visualized dream onto a piece of paper, and then from a piece of paper to an actual reality, witnessing the effect of this transformative process on the lives of others is among Kris's greatest motivations.

"You put so much time into something, and then it all pays off on the day you open that business and see how it impacts peoples' lives through creating jobs and building communities," he reflects. "When you've had a vision for years and you see the day that you're able to follow it through to fruition—now that's a phenomenal feeling." Through his steadfast commitment to positive and lasting growth, Hart Strategic Enterprises is sure to continue opening doors to new businesses and new opportunities for many years to come.

Christopher Helmrath

The Culture of a Connector

As a child, Chris Helmrath always knew he was loved. His father, a neonatologist who also graduated from a top ten graduate business school, however had his own unique way of showing it. "He's not the kind of person you sit around with on a Sunday, watching sappy movies and talking about your girlfriend," Chris laughs. "With him, it was always about achieving your potential and not accepting average results. We were forbidden from getting a 'C' on our report cards and could not watch television unless we read books, which he would quiz us over to make sure we had done a good job."

Indeed, Chris and his siblings learned the value of a strong work ethic from the beginning, always understanding that failure was not an option. Now the managing partner of the northern Virginia office of the SC&H Group, LLC, Chris has cultivated this lesson over the years into an enduring and powerful frame of mind that lends a unique edge to all that he does. "I'm not willing to accept mediocrity," he readily acknowledges. "I push and push and push."

Chris's upbringing, however, was by no means all work and no heart. In fact, he remembers the stories of his grandfather's examples of unwavering kindness as among the most influential lessons of his life. His grandfather had dropped out of school in the eighth grade to support his mother and sister after his father's untimely death, later overcoming all odds when he was named President of the Passenger Division of the Illinois Central Railroad. He was also one of the original founders of the Sugar Bowl in New Orleans.

Upon Chris's graduation from high school, his grandparents gave him a framed print entitled, "The Art of Getting Along," which advocated compassion, friendliness, and patience in all that one does. "He knew everybody in New Orleans and he shook everyone's hand," Chris remembers. "It was remarkable how he connected in the business community without a formal education, accomplishing such tremendous things with his charisma and personality." Today, Chris's leadership philosophy unites the work ethic learned from his father with the benevolence learned from his grandfather and lends an invaluable contribution to SC&H, both in terms of its culture and its bottom line.

SC&H is a conglomerate of 265 financial professionals who specialize in developing accounting, tax, management consulting, and investment banking solutions for an extensive range of clients. Founded in 1991 in Baltimore, the firm has offices in the Baltimore and D.C. metropolitan areas with a smaller office in Atlanta, and it serves clients across the Unites States. The firm's revenues are proportioned equally between its audit, tax, and consulting practices, and its revenue growth rate has averaged over 25 percent annually since its inception.

Since Chris signed on with the firm in 2005, SC&H has grown by 2.5 times across the firm as a whole. The Tysons office, however, has followed a different trend, reporting fewer than 10 employees when Chris started and now clocking in at just fewer than 40. "We see this office as probably the greatest growth opportunity SC&H has right now," he reports. "Thus, we're very focused on investing, hiring, and getting in the market to grow as much as possible."

When Chris began with SC&H's Baltimore group, he had no idea he would later be asked to serve as managing partner for northern Virginia. Certainly his business development potential was impressive and untapped, having taught in 2 graduate schools for fifteen years and also building a strong presence in financial services and in the non-profit realm for his contributions to the surrounding community. Such alliances speak to a skill set often lacking in the public accounting world—one that blends the diverse challenges of managing people, managing growth, and maintaining market presence.

Chris's career in the financial services industry first began with the acquisition of banks for a Fortune 100 company based in Chicago, originally coming to Northern Virginia to buy failed S&Ls and build the brand out into Maryland. Early on, he was quickly taken under the wing of the regional President, who became a trusted mentor by opening many doors for Chris along his path toward success. "John gave me opportunities that a 23-year-old should never have," Chris laughs now. "Knowing I wanted to go to graduate school, he sat me down in his office one day and said he wouldn't promote me until I got my MBA."

Two days later, Chris took the GMAT and quickly enrolled at Loyola University, graduating first in his class of several hundred despite balancing school and work with the challenges of becoming a father. Though Chris eventually departed from that industry after deciding that it held no long-term viability for him, he never forgot the invaluable tools he had collected through the experience. "I'm a connector," he remarks now, commenting on his respect for the role of relationships in personal growth. "I have learned that every relationship has a purpose in your life, even if you may not understand it today. Never forget who people are, because it is people that will help you get where you're going."

Chris later joined the accounting and tax group of American Express, which was the ninth largest accounting firm in the U.S. at the time. Such opportunities lent him a tremendous wealth of knowledge, not only in the technical aspects of his trade, but also in employee development, training, and group management. The resulting alchemy of expertise would prove to make all the difference for Chris and his career at SC&H. "If you watch any business evolve, you need people that are growers and people who are maintainers," he points out. "I'm not a maintainer, I'm a grower."

Drawing upon his extensive and textured expertise in investment banking, Chris now serves as President and Principal of SC&H's FINRA-regulated merger and acquisition services practice, SC&H Capital. This entity entails ten professionals focusing in investment banking, business valuation, strategic planning, debt, and capital raise, offering a truly unique service in the field and serving as a testament to the creative, outside-the-box culture that SC&H is proud to call its own.

Above all else, SC&H is about culture. "Culture is our number one corporate objective," explains Chris. "It's the first litmus test in examining any next step for us, be it a possible acquisition or something else. If it doesn't fit within our culture, we won't do it." Through its innovative and imaginative method of managing people and creating environments and career paths, the firm challenges the traditional mold of the accounting industry's accepted firm structure in virtually all that it does, and this capacity toward originality has won SC&H an employee turnover rate which is about a third of the industry-wide figure.

Respect and integrity are of paramount importance for Chris and his team, and this entails a very unique attitude toward both clients and employees alike. "At SC&H, no employee has billable hour goals," Chris reports. "Our job as partners is to monitor and manage across the line and make sure we're delivering to our clients what they need. We focus on not burning anybody out and are continually assessing every situation to ensure that we have the right resources at work on each job." This attitude allows the firm to skirt the bureaucracy that so often strangles the work-life balance at other firms, engendering an atmosphere of collegiality and equality.

This company culture allows the partners at SC&H to develop lasting and genuine relationships with their clients just as diligently as they develop products and solutions that work. "We want the client to be as delighted about the work product we've done as they are about working with us," Chris explains. "Churning out employees and clients is simply not what we do here. At the beginning and end of each day, we ask ourselves, are we doing the right thing?"

In ensuring that the answer to this question is a perpetual and resounding *yes*, Chris sees himself as a servant just as much as he sees himself a leader. Honoring the mantra, "Do what ought to be done but would not have been done unless I did it," he holds that there is no job he's unwilling to do and no statement he's unwilling to make. "Everything we touch leaves a mark," Chris observes. "That's what I enjoy most. If you can help someone see something, or see through something, or think better and differently about something, that's my favorite part of the day."

What makes Chris's philosophy so unique, then, is its keen awareness of each person's ability to affect the world and the essence of responsibility that necessarily accompanies that reality. "No one human being can motivate another," Chris points out. "You can only create an environment in which one motivates himself. We all have the ability to create an environment that affects others, and using this power to maximize someone's potential—that's what it's all about for me."

If his father imparted the value of work ethic and his grandfather imparted the value of kindness, Chris draws from his mother the passion it takes to truly affect environments in a meaningful and lasting way—through education. "With a father who taught in a medical school and a mother who was a kindergarten teacher, teaching became such a critical part of my world," he remarks now. When he first began teaching at Loyola University, it quickly became apparent that teaching was a true passion—a way to give back.

Chris's teaching career spanned across 2 graduate business schools and 19 years, where he ultimately ran the MBA Capstone Program for the Carey Business School at Johns Hopkins University. Reflecting back on instances when prior students of his would approach him outside of the classroom to let him know how meaningful his lessons had been, Chris considers such moments to be lessons in themselves. "That's a 'Wow, I did something right' moment," he emphasizes. In 2003, the Johns Hopkins University named him the top teacher in the business school by granting him the Excellence in Teaching Award, and he considers this to be one of his greatest professional achievements.

"At SC&H, we believe that giving back is a fundamental piece of who we are. I was very fortunate, having a family that taught me so much and now being able to give back through teaching."

So, when Chris is speaking to a classroom full of entrepreneurs poised to venture into the workforce, what invaluable idioms does he choose to impart? Indeed, the resounding message that threads through each life lesson he strives to impart is the importance of attitude. Through attitude, one can grasp work ethic by wanting something more than the next person and acting accordingly. Through attitude, one can grasp heart by treating others as you would want to be treated. And through attitude, one can take the raw materials of life and mold environments that engender success, happiness, and progress, both for others and for themselves. "So many people are frozen when confronted with ambiguity," he says. "Dealing constructively with ambiguity is really all about attitude." By wielding attitude in this manner, one can hope to enter the business world with grace and gusto, fervor and poise.

Greg Jones

The Business of Team Spirit

Growing up in a blue collar town in Western Pennsylvania, Greg Jones may have been the short fat kid, but that all changed in eighth grade when he hit a major growth spurt and suddenly found himself over six feet tall and chock-full of athletic talent. He played wide receiver for the varsity football team during his sophomore year, moving up the ranks as a running back and linebacker by the time he was a junior. He sought out by college recruiters across the country but decided to play for Penn State, mastering the concept of team and embodying the power of hard work while staying close to home.

"Then, after college and after playing for the Eagles for one season, the real world set in," Greg recalls. "Do you keep striving for the NFL dream, or do you go with it? It's a humbling world out here, especially coming from where I came from." He remembers the first several years out of school as being tremendously formidable, but he soon learned that those same tenets of team and hard work could be leveraged in the business world just as he had leveraged them on the football field.

"I learned that people in the business world had successes and failures just the same, and I realized I could play in that world too," Greg continues. After spending time in corporate America and learning how to climb that ladder, he soon realized there was no reason he couldn't pursue another dream: the goal of running his own business. Now the CEO of BookKeeping Express, the nation's only franchise model for outsourced bookkeeping and financial intelligence consulting, Greg's entrepreneurial spirit takes the idea of team to a whole new level.

BookKeeping Express was originally founded in 1984 in Southern California by Roy Graboff, who had wanted to start up a small practice to get out of corporate America. Graboff grew the firm through a license model that would grant licensees the right to use the firm's software program and name. Through training licensees in this manner, Roy and his team grew the company to 150 locations throughout the U.S., establishing a strong brand and national presence by the mid nineties.

In 2007, Greg and his business partner were looking for an investment and stumbled across a BookKeeping Express licensee in Virginia. Greg reports that the light bulb went on immediately, and as they investigated the organization, they admired the fact that it serviced the largest business segment in the U.S. with mandatory product offerings whose necessity and value wouldn't ebb and flow with the protean tides of the economy. "My interest was piqued," Greg remembers. "We did our due diligence, bought the company, and moved the headquarters to Northern Virginia in 2007. By January of 2008, BookKeeping Express Enterprises was opened for business."

Launching the business for franchising was a long and grueling dance with the Federal Trade Commission that didn't end until August of 2008, but it was well worth the effort, and Greg has been franchising the business ever since. "The organization had very little involvement with its network of locations back when we were simply licensing," Greg explains, "whereas franchising is the complete opposite." While the number of BookKeeping Express licenses slowly gave way to attrition, slipping from its peak of 150 down to roughly 22 today, BookKeeping Express currently boasts 26 franchisees in 22 different states, with two locations in Canada and one master developer invested in North Carolina. Greg predicts this number will double in 2011 and again in 2012, with a goal of reaching 100 franchisees throughout North America by the beginning of 2013.

"When you strip it all down, our mission is essentially to meet with entrepreneurs that wish to build a company and match them with our system," Greg explains. "We help people to meet their goals and dreams of expanding their wealth and their life options. This mission—this premise of 'why'—is a central concept in our organization. We've built a turnkey business model with everything from ongoing business training to a full IT structure so that our franchisees can focus on their immediate roles."

In this sense, BookKeeping Express forms a team relationship with each of its franchisees, and nobody knows team spirit better than Greg. "Franchising is a team sport," he says with a laugh. "Because you get the model, the program, the marketing material, and everything else in place, it's like you're starting your business at the forty yard line. All the franchisee has to do is apply the sense, the skill set, and the business savvy. They only have to take the model and run with it." In that sense, franchisees save hundreds of thousands of dollars in startup costs, and are thus able to build more successful and stable operations from the get-go.

From the beginning, Greg and his team have focused on minimizing costs for their franchisees while maximizing efficiency through the utilization of cutting edge technology. By doing more with less and reaping the benefits of a paperless environment, BookKeeping Express is able to bring the skills and the resources that allow their entrepreneurs to maximize the virtual realm. The firm also utilizes a third party marketing firm based in Chicago, among the best in the franchise business, to brand the company throughout North America.

At the same time, this marketing firm represents and promotes BookKeeping Express's individual franchisees within their respective territories, connecting them with the newspaper, radio, magazine, and television presences they need to create buzz-worthy exposure. To supplement these efforts, one BookKeeping Express staff member is assigned to each new franchisee for the franchise's first 18 weeks of operation, providing coaching and mentoring to ensure that the program is being rolled out effectively.

Considering the strong current of entrepreneurialism that seems to permeate Greg's bloodstream, it comes as quite a surprise that he didn't have a lot of successful entrepreneurial mentors in his past. "Early on, I always wanted to be the leader, the owner, the captain," he remarks. "Having achieved what I did in athletics, I know you don't get there just by hoping and wishing. It takes a lot of hard work and energy, and these lessons definitely helped to prepare me for the journey ahead. If you let a few punches shake your focus from what the company is all about, you aren't going to be successful."

After earning his business degree, Greg worked as part of a management training program with Lowes Corporation before entering the Telecom world, which was just heating up at the time. He sold hardware for the Harris Corporation in the D.C. metro area to the federal government, advancing up the corporate ladder from salesperson to sales manager to sales director through the early 1990s. He then joined a little Chicago-based telecom service company called LCI, revitalizing it until it was deemed among the best telecom service companies in the country.

Though he held an esteemed management position, Greg and his wife wanted to move their young family out of Chicago, so he accepted a position as VP of sales for an international telecom company based out of D.C. called Primus Telecommunications. "Through these efforts, I had the opportunity to see what happens at the top versus what happens below the top as a company goes public," Greg remarks now. "It spurred my interest and got me wanting to start a company of my own."

Thus, in 1997, he and two partners launched an organization called Net Results. Targeting Fortune 1000 Companies, Net Results served to reduce their clients' telecommunications costs and was compensated by splitting the difference. Greg and his partners grew the firm until they sold it in 2002, at which point his adventurous nature had taken an interest in franchising and real estate. He and his partners bought the franchise rights for several Five Guys restaurants, launching the popular chain's first Florida location. Subsequent to that endeavor, Greg found himself helping a firm in Alexandria, Virginia, that specialized in developing franchise concepts. Noting the prevalence of company owners with an abundance of passion and interest but lacking in the expansive skill set necessary to start a business from scratch, Greg realized he was faced with an opportunity to really make a difference. "At that point, I knew it was time to make a leap," he remembers. "We decided to take it to a national scale, and the rest is history."

In advising young entrepreneurs entering the workforce today, Greg advocates for a broad-spectrum mentality that encourages advanced planning and foresight. "Kids these days have such a short window, but I would suggest that they try to look out a little further and really ask themselves what they want to be and what excites them," he says. "There's the old adage that says you should do what you're passionate about. It's hard to figure that out as a kid, but try."

In examining where one's passion might lie, Greg suggests looking two or three steps past the entry-level position in that field, quizzing people who hold such positions about their daily lives to acquire a better understanding of what it's really like. "Unfortunately, kids come out today needing to get a job and often have to accept positions that are far off base from what they want to do," he acknowledges. "Don't give up on your dream, but instead try to develop a timeline for how to get back to what you really want to do. It's all about having a game plan."

Regardless of whether you've arrived at where you want to be or you're still working your way toward that goal, Greg emphasizes the importance of cultivating and obeying that inner drive that keeps one focused. "When I need motivation, I look in the mirror," he says. "I hate the idea of not succeeding, and because of that, there's no one that drives me more than I, myself, do."

Indeed, pursuing one's goals is not so much a competition between one's self and others, but rather a competition between one's own success or failure. By aiming high and working as a team with the people in one's life, success is made possible not only for yourself, but for others as well. "With BookKeeping Express, I love that my goal is achieved in helping our franchisees achieve their goals," he says. "This means that everyone's heart and passion has to be in it a hundred and twenty percent."Through this philosophy, Greg and his affiliates have the opportunity to partake in a success that, collectively, is much bigger than the dream of any single individual, and much more rewarding as well.

Dick Kettler

Mastering the Test of Time

In 1978, with his graduation from Georgetown Law imminent, Dick Kettler felt that taking the position of Associate Counsel at premier DC real estate firm Wilkes Artis was a natural next step. Beyond the fact that Dick had clerked there while working towards his JD at Georgetown, the Kettler family had been immersed in DC-area real estate since the 1930s, and had resided in the area since the late nineteenth century. Dick's father, Clarence, had been the president and founder of the two-decades old Kettler Brothers building company, a group whose partners and employees spanned the Kettler extended family. Dick graduated in May of 1978, passed the DC bar that summer, and became an associate attorney at Wilkes Artis by Thanksgiving of that year.

Born in 1953 as the first of seven children, the underpinnings of his career path were fixed at an early age. "With all those kids it was kind of a madhouse," Dick remembers. His father's building company was founded only a year before he was born, but he didn't feel that he was necessarily wedded to the business. "There wasn't this sense of sitting down at the family table, or having that father-son thing, to talk about the family business. It didn't happen," he says. Still, Dick paid attention. "As a kid you're always watching your father, and to a boy the father is a big deal. As a kid, he was my hero."

Thus, he always thought he might somehow end up in the building industry, though he doesn't describe himself as a builder. "If you gave me a hammer and nails, it wouldn't be a good situation!" he laughs. "Still, I thought I would get into the building business even though I didn't know when or why or how."

By the start of 1979, the closest that Dick Kettler, associate counsel, had come to working in the home building business himself was a one-off renovation job he executed with friends and relatives in 1975 between graduating from Brown and starting at Georgetown. Around the same time he had an exploratory conversation with his father in which Clarence strongly encouraged his son to go to graduate school and pledged to support him there. Four years later, there he was, with a JD from Georgetown and a promising position at a DC law firm.

Despite the many merits of this opportunity, Dick actually found himself closer to the business of his father than he had ever been before when his cousin, Kip Forlines, founded Kettler Forlines Homes in 1978. The two then had several long conversations about Dick joining the company. Though he was in the midst of launching his career as a real estate attorney and was very pleased with his new work, which would have him learning alongside several very talented attorneys at the time, Dick can still recall the persistence of that lingering thought that his future lay in homebuilding and developing. Realizing this thought, Kip convinced him to leave his law firm and join Kettler Forlines Homes in April of 1979.

Kettler Forlines owes much of its current success to its rich and extensive history of integration in the DC metro area. Indeed, about a century earlier, the first generation of Washington DC Kettlers had set up shop in the meat business as one of the most prominent presences in the Washington industry at the time, selling to hundreds of merchants and to numerous area hotels and restaurants. Decades later, on the eve of the Great Depression, the Kettler Brothers left the meat business behind. Dick's grandfather Clifford and his brothers then entered the real estate market with the purchase of first one and then half a dozen apartment buildings in 1930, which they then operated as landlords into the forties. Clarence, Dick's father, also worked there briefly. A year after Clifford's death, Clarence started the Kettler Brothers building company in 1952.

"It's a rather unique family history in Washington," he says, "with every generation being successful. Typically, in these family case studies, it's seldom that they'll get beyond a couple generations. Things tend to happen and sometimes go to worms." Further, Dick sees particular significance in the fact that there hasn't been one Kettler Brothers company that each generation of Kettlers has inherited. "It's not like we tried to have one business to pass down through a hundred years," he observes. Rather, the Kettlers have experienced a series of successes across several generations. While it's tempting to try to divine an inherited trait or some other kind of success-in-the-blood, Dick is hesitant to find a driving reason behind his family's continuing successes.

"I think that originally, back in the 1880s, my great-grandfather and his family were just middle-class folks trying to survive," he explains. "Then my grandfather took over the meat business when his father died around 1919. It would be easy to say that this was the start of a family dynasty or something like that, but really, when the opportunity to get into real estate came along, it was business acumen and not inheritance that led to more success in our family."

All that Dick will allow is that a deeply ingrained independence and work ethic figures prominently into this success. "My father did see his own father work for himself, and each Kettler generation has had that," he remarks. Dick says that although he never had that close father-son relationship in which Clarence revealed the mysteries of his success, as a son he was always watching his father and taking mental notes. Recounting the story of his family in DC, Dick sees the pattern of entrepreneurship emerging from "some kind of family rule" where each generation pays close attention to the one prior, then sets out to be their own bosses.

"It's like osmosis," Dick muses. "I wasn't always deliberative and purposeful in where I was going to go. I had those skills, but I would go with the flow a bit." Reflecting back on his decision to join Kettler Forlines in its infancy to work for himself and be his own boss, Dick now feels that going with the flow, listening to that "lingering thought", and following his gut has ultimately led him to the best-fitting career he could have hoped for.

Kettler Forlines's first real enterprise was to build 24 townhouses at the Hidden Valley ski resort near Pittsburgh, and this project had already been launched when Dick came on board. Kip Forlines was in Pennsylvania working that project, and Dick assumed the role of drawing business back in the DC area. Initially he was working out of an office that was six by eight feet with one phone. "We weren't starting at a very robust time, and we had to go through these 15% interest rate mortgages," Dick says. "But our family had and continues to maintain relationships in this town, and opportunities presented themselves."

After buying a few lots in Centreville, Virginia and joint venturing their development with another cousin of his, Bob Kettler, Kettler Forlines then quickly moved on more properties in Silver Spring and elsewhere, starting what became a huge ramp-up during the '80s. They built staff and infrastructure and expanded into two offices, then later into their own suite down the street. "I think we doubled our size every year from '79 to '89," Dick recalls.

The relationships that he and his family developed over decades of home-building in the region were instrumental in the success of Kettler

Forlines during this time, not merely in terms of business relationships and connections that led to building opportunities, but also friendships with leaders in the industry who were able to mentor Dick and offer guidance to the young building company through various economic conditions. Further, the solid Kettler reputation allowed him to get his foot in the door in the beginning, which allowed Kettler Forlines to establish its own reputation as a dominant force in the making. "My job," Dick says, "was to go around soliciting people and trying to pull it all together. I would find an opportunity, then go around and start asking questions, then put together a picture of what we needed to do and to give it some guidance. Relationships were key in this process."

In 1989, Kettler Forlines hit a peak at 120 employees and revenues near $50 million. "Life was looking really good," Dick recalls with a grin. However, by the late 1980s the housing market had become overheated, and the lending environment hit to a sudden wall due to the savings and loan crisis and subsequent recession in the early '90s. "In the '80s we were basically banking off of our family's reputation," Dick explains. "At the start, especially, we didn't have much beyond seed money loaned to us from my father, which we had paid back before 1990." Kettler Forlines had several million in unsecured lines of credit across three banks in Maryland. Able to borrow without mortgages or construction inspections and their associated fees and bureaucratic time-sinks had fueled their initial success, but that period was coming to a close.

"1990 came and all hell broke loose," Dick says. "Until then the banking business had been very much based on relationships. We had phenomenal credit and never should have had it based on what we really started with. But our reputation and our relationships allowed us that initial chance, and then our accomplishments spoke for themselves."

Kettler Forlines "limped along" through the '90s, trying to tread water. They ran a bad project that almost ended the enterprise, but they worked through it. By 1997 into 1998, things picked up again, and Dick describes the ride up from '97 to 2005 and early 2006 as a highly interesting time. "We had extraordinary demand for new homes, and we had to limit new sales in order to keep up with our production schedules," he recalls. "We all worked very hard to keep pace with that demand."

Though the appreciation in housing through 2005 was phenomenal, Kettler Forlines then had a series of "canary in the coal mine" incidents that allowed them to sense that something was coming. As Hurricane Katrina devastated the nation and the impending depression began to rear its head, Dick remembers thinking, "This is going to be a lot worse than people think. We were right there, taking the pulse every day."

Since the onset of the worst American economic downturn since the Great Depression, Kettler Forlines has certainly suffered along with the rest of the nation. Going from 120 employees down to 18 with revenue in 2010 at $9 million, down from $50 million in 1989 without adjusting for inflation, things have certainly changed. However, Dick looks forward to the future with several creative ideas to get his company back to a reasonable program. He describes the events in the housing market as an "impressive death spiral. Prices go down, then there are foreclosures, and appraisals go down in those neighborhoods, and it's very hard to find a bottom." But Kettler Forlines does have something going for them in that they've been through a cyclical crisis before and survived.

"We know how to get through this," Dick states with impressive fortitude. Indeed, Kettler Forlines has built roughly four thousand homes across one hundred communities in four states. They've won 85 major industry awards, and at one point were among the top 400 building companies nationwide. But Kettler Forlines will not be resting on its laurels by any means. "We have to get into the mindset that this is a start-up business," Dick asserts. "Coming in we have a lot of experience, but we're starting in a new market and we have to behave as such."

There may be less land and tougher approval and credit environments, but Dick is still confident. "I'm not merely a builder," he remarks. I'm an attorney, an entrepreneur, a business manager, a leader—*whatever*."

He understands that getting through this era in American history is going to take more than an established and successful home-building company: it's going to take a finely tuned intuition for history and practiced hands. Fortunately for Dick and for Kettler Forlines, they possess both qualities in spades.

David Keuhner

It's About The Experience

If one of the basic tenets of business success is to find a need and fill it, David Keuhner is right on point. As founder and Chief Executive Officer of Destination Cellars, he has created a business that fills a void in the hospitality industry—a void that Keuhner personally experienced.

"We had a love of wine and one of the places that I always wanted to visit was Bordeaux," Keuhner reveals.

Keuhner began contacting various wineries in Bordeaux to see if he could create an experience for himself to visit the chateaus and meet the winemakers. "I wanted to gain access. It's like getting courtside seats to a sports game. If you could gain access to Chateau Lafite-Rothschild (regarded as one of the world's greatest clarets) what would those walls say?"

The task proved considerably daunting. Many of his emails were not responded to and when they were, the first question was usually "Who are you?" Keuhner also searched for a company that could arrange every aspect of his dream trip, but to no avail. Because of the less than warm response in Bordeaux, Keuhner and his wife focused on wineries in Napa Valley.

It was in the mid-90's when Keuhner and his wife first experienced what Destination Cellars now regularly offers its clients: opportunities to meet directly with winemakers, have private dinners at chateaus and purchase wine that may not be available to the public. Out of his own desire for a one-of-a-kind trip to a winery, he has built a business providing access to the world of wine and created similar memorable experiences for his clients.

"Destination Cellars provides a completely customized service. We help our clients put the pieces of the puzzle together," states Keuhner, "If it has to do with the world of wine, we can help".

The services that Destination Cellars offers are designed to meet the needs of organizational and individual clients. The first service is wine experiential travel, where customers can have private visits to over 175 wineries in 10 countries around the world. A high level of careful attention is given to clients seeking wine experiential services.

"Because everybody is different, we find out what our clients really want to get out of their trip. Some are more interested in cooking with wine, some want to taste a variety of wines and some want to learn the science behind winemaking. Others simply want to gain access to wineries in order to take in the rich history and culture of the locale."

The second service offered is helping clients acquire wine. As a licensed retailer, importer and wholesaler, Destination Cellars works directly with winery partners to procure incredible products. "Collecting fine wine ranks up there with collecting art or cars, and it operates along the same principles", shares Keuhner.

The third service offered is wine event management. Clients hire Destination Cellars to 'bring the wine to them' for private social events, business meetings and board retreats.

Keuhner's interest in travel may have been cultivated by his growing up in a career military family. Both of his grandfathers held high-ranking military positions, one as a Colonel in the Air Force and the other as a Colonel in the Army, while his father was an Army major who served two tours in Viet Nam. As a teen, Keuhner assumed that he would follow in their footsteps, career-wise, but when he shared his plans with his grandfather, Keuhner was surprised when the 32-year veteran said, "You don't want to do that. That was my choice. You need to go out and create a life of your own."

It was during this time that Keuhner was first introduced to the world of wine. His uncle was the sommelier for the 21 Club, a renowned restaurant in New York City, which had one of the largest wine cellars in the state. Keuhner relished exploring the wine cellars in the restaurant where they stored bottles belonging to VIP's, such as President Richard Nixon, and unclaimed bottles that were being stored by U.S. soldiers who intended to share the wine with their children when they became of age. These 'wine stories' came alive for him and this piqued Keuhner's interest in learning more about wine.

After receiving his associate degree in Business, Keuhner held several jobs in the hospitality industry. During his time at Ruth's Chris Steak House, he rose through the ranks to become the youngest General Manger, overseeing three locations in the DC metro area and bringing in annual sales of $5 million.

Keuhner's next position was as the head of the regional sales team for JTECH Communications, which provided electronic pager services for restaurants. Keuhner covered the area from Pennsylvania to Florida and the company grew to serve over 75,000 restaurants in the United States. The founder of company, Dave Miller, was like a second father to Keuhner who lost his own father at a young age.

After JTECH Communications, Keuhner was hired as the East Coast Regional Director for Opentable.com, which is now the leading online reservations company in the world and then served as Vice

President for Fishbowl, an online marketing agency, where he built the company from start-up to $15 million in sales and from three employees to over 100 in the first five years. Keuhner learned a great deal from working in these entrepreneurial environments, and with his wife's blessing, he decided to start his own business.

"When we started in 2007, we literally traveled the world. We made all of our agreements with winery partners in person so that we could stand by what we promised our customers. The winery needed to know what kind of experience we wanted for our customers. This was about creating relationships, not talking via email."

Destination Cellars got off to a good start. Their first sale was $11,850 for arranging a client visit to Bordeaux. Despite the language barrier, the client had an amazing adventure.

Though the market turn in 2008 slowed down the business, Keuhner stayed the course and began to develop connections with organizations that have large numbers of consumers who want to experience the world of wine. Keuhner also launched an online component where member organizations' clients can have access to specialized wine services.

"The wine industry has grown over the years and is now a $30 billion industry with every state in the US currently producing wine. Last year 140 new wineries were licensed and bonded in the state of Virginia alone and wine sales in the US are the highest in the world (per capita)," says Keuhner, "Wine is becoming a social status, the exclusivity of a product and the social experience that attracts buyers. People want to say 'I have this in my collection' or 'Only 200 cases were made and I have one of them'. In fact, Cornell University now offers a complete wine course for students about to embark into the work world."

With this tremendous growth and the increasing global interest in wine, Destination Cellars' future looks bright.

"What's happening in the wine industry has been pretty exciting to witness," says Keuhner. "We get to see both sides because we work directly with wineries and the consumer."

Keuhner's advice to young people just getting into the work world is simple, 'Don't ever give up'. He also suggests a three-prong strategy of determination, dedication and believing in yourself.

"You have to get clear in your own mind that you can do it, that you can succeed. Believe in yourself, whether you want to become a chef, an accountant, or own a business. Learn to set goals for yourself. It can be a simple goal, but you do need to have one."

Keuhner speaks fondly of the people who have supported him in his personal and professional life. "In addition to my mom and grandparents, a neighbor, Donald, took me under his wing and treated me like a son. Professionally, I try to surround myself with good people and have been strongly influenced by Allen Cage, Justin Wender, and Chad MacDonald (the first investor in Destination Cellars)."

There are two things that make David Keuhner tick, and they are both found prominently displayed in his office. The first is a photo of his father surrounded by award medals from serving in Vietnam. The second is a photo of his family.

"That's what motivates me to be successful, and hopefully I will achieve something that I can pass along to my kids. In fact, the best compliment I ever received was on Father's Day when the Assistant Coach on our baseball team told me 'You're the best dad I've ever known'. If my kids will think that, I've done a good job."

The importance that David Keuhner places on family, sharing experiences, bringing people together and being passionate about what you enjoy is fully reflected in both his personal and professional life. He set out to create memories for himself and found himself creating memories for others. With David Keuhner, it's not just travel; it's about the experience.

BERNHARDT

WEALTH MANAGEMENT

Richard Knop

The Evolution of Bliss

When children contemplate what they want to be when they grow up, they are often told that they should follow their bliss, and young Richard Knop was committed to doing just that. "Growing up in Indiana, I was absolutely fascinated by the fossils hidden in the limestone quarries in our town," Rick remembers now. "I decided I would become a paleontologist."

This resolve held, and through his freshman year at Indiana University, he did indeed major in geology with a focus in paleontology. Pursuing a well-rounded liberal arts curriculum, however, he also sampled courses from other disciplines, including several prelaw classes. His mother had always urged him to consider law, as her father had been an attorney, and his father in turn had been the first patent lawyer in America.

Rick was doing fairly well in school during his sophomore year when he received the sudden and tragic news that his mother had died.

"I can't say why exactly, but I turned on a dime," he recalls. "Frankly, it was the catalyst that changed the rest of my life." Rick immediately switched his course of study from paleontology to prelaw, and his performance rocketed from average to impeccable. It was safe to say that his bliss had evolved.

"I decided I wanted to go to law school, so I buckled down and spent the rest of my college career earning the A's that would allow me to do that." Now a managing partner of FedCap Partners, LLC, Rick may not be pursuing his original childhood dream job, but his remarkable success, fulfillment, and impact are a testament to the idea that passion need not be stagnant, but should instead continue to expand and enrich just as we, as people, do.

Launched on February 7, 2010, FedCap is a small private equity fund with $30 million in assets exclusively focused on making minority equity growth capital investments in government defense contractors drawing between $10 and $75 million in revenue. They serve an array of clients from diverse fields that include cyber security, intelligence, battlefield digitization, healthcare, IT, energy and environment, all of which provide very high-end solutions in areas in which FedCap predicts the budget will be stable or increasing. "There's never been an equity fund like this," Rick says proudly.

In what ways, exactly, is FedCap so unique from its competitors? The answer is rooted deep in the organization's history, extending back to a time when it was nothing more than an idea. Then the owner of The Windsor Group, among the leading investment banks in the defense contracting industry, Rick had spotted a vacuum. "Private equity groups had been very much focused on that industry, but they all want to take controlling or 100 percent ownership positions," he points out. "None of them were interested in making minority growth capital investments, especially for smaller government contractors, and none of them have really taken the time to know the industry like we do."

Rick's background is in the transactional financial side of the business, while his partner, Leslee Beluccie, focuses on the company's operations management. Prior to coming to FedCap, she held prominent positions with IBM, setting her apart as a senior executive in the government contracting industry. Both Rick and Leslee bring over 20 years of expertise in the government contracting industry to the table and together own FedCap Advisors, which is the managing partner of FedCap Partners.

"The kind of company we're focused on investing in is very solutions-oriented and doing important work for the country," Rick describes. "Ideally, the owner would also like to sell within two to five years." FedCap, then, offers minority equity growth capital and advice that can take these companies to the next level and prepare them for the ultimate liquidity event—an opportunity that doesn't happen easily in today's financial services climate. 'Typically, these companies earn between $20 and $40 million in revenue, and in order to advance beyond the small-business mold, they must remake their infrastructure," he continues. "We take the mystery out of how to do this, providing both the capital and the advice needed to make it happen."

Since their doors officially opened on March 1, Rick and his team have reviewed over 200 companies. They made their first investment in September of that year in a company called IntelliWare Systems, which performs mission architecture for counter-terrorism initiatives. Essentially connecting the dots between law enforcement and intelligence, and their principle clients are homeland security and the FBI.

Since then, FedCap has closed on an investment in a $40 million Department of Energy IT company (GAITS), and another in a $15 million intelligence agency contractor (GRS). Additionally, FedCap purchased 100 percent of Point One, a cyber security company for intelligence and defense.

Just as FedCap isn't your average equity fund, Rick isn't your average equity fund manager. A true self-starter, he has always been one to find his own way, and while that path has been anything but straight, it's as if each stage added an important feature to his repertoire and expertise that have led him to where he is today, so far from the little house in the little town in which he was raised.

A Midwesterner in heart and spirit, Rick's humble upbringing and friendly nature exude from his tone and mannerisms. He mowed lawns every summer to earn money for college, supplementing that income with additional revenue from his own painting contracting business and from construction jobs. Rick also worked his way through law school when he enrolled at George Washington University, where his mother's father and grandfather had received their legal educations. He secured a job with the legal advisor of the State Department, which he held from his first year's second semester to his third year's end.

Upon graduation with a J.D. with honors, Rick initially focused on international law and, as a supplement to his legal education, earned acceptance to Harvard's MBA program. He was wrapping up with his third year coursework, and the future seemed secure and promising when he rang his father to tell him the good news. Mr. Knop, however, delivered tidings that would again forever alter the course of Rick's life. "The Draft Board had a lottery yesterday, and your number was called," explained Mr. Knop, a World War II veteran. "Like me, you're going to have to serve your country."

With a young wife, a child on the way, and law school loans to pay off, Rick joined the Army Reserve and earned a commission as a first lieutenant and spent six years in the Reserves. He later assumed a position as a Legislative Assistant to the then-ranking Republican on the Foreign Affairs Committee—what he refers to as his first "real" job.

"I have been called the quiet catalyst, and that's how I've always viewed myself," Rick reflects. "On Capitol Hill, I had the opportunity to synthesize complex issues, personalities, and viewpoints and to unite them on a common ground. I weave a web that brings people together without putting me in the middle and help parties agree on complex issues." Highly skilled and creative at assembling legislation and accruing bipartisan support, he developed a thirst and passion for the entrepreneurial act of creation that would serve him well in years to come.

After six years on the Hill, Rick uprooted his family and moved to Florida at the invitation of the Congressman he was working for at the time. The Representative planned to run for governor several years later, and he wanted Rick to work at his law firm in Orlando with the intention of appointing him his Secretary of Commerce if he were to be elected. The Congressman never actually ran, but Rick had the opportunity to practice law for the first time. He eventually accepted a position with a DC-based firm called Wyatt and Saltstein, and the Knops returned North once more despite the comfortable life they had built for themselves in Florida.

While the international law he studied in school proved fascinating yet sometimes ephemeral and his Capitol Hill experience imparted expertise on a wide scope of subjects, it wasn't until he was actually on the job in the 1980s that Rick earned a solid working understanding of business, performing a number of international business transactions. "I became extremely interested in business as I became involved in complex business transactions," he reports. "You pick up by osmosis what the drivers are in such situations."

Once he had worked in law for a decade or so, it dawned on Rick that the fundamental process of law was more about documentation and technicality than it was about catalyzing and synthesizing. "As I practiced law, I found myself constantly looking for opportunities to put businesses together and create things," Rick explains. "I really wanted to be involved in the transactions from day one. That's why I decided to launch a company that would allow me to be a full-time dealmaker."

The company that resulted from this desire—the Windsor Group—was established in 1992 and truly flourished into a business paradigm that has withstood the test of time. Helping clients as they sought to sell, refinance, recapitalize, expand, or take a company public, it has shaped the industry into what it is today and continues to be a widely replicated model. "In the middle market like this, you're essentially creating new companies and new paradigms out of whole cloth," says Rick, words rich with the electricity of the process. "It's highly creative, multidisciplinary, nuanced, and academic. It's a little different than a large investment bank on Wall Street."

When BB&T approached Windsor in 2005 with a proposal to turn it into the preeminent investment and commercial bank focusing on the government contracting industry, Rick and his partner agreed, and Rick stayed on until his last earn-out payment was made in 2009. Feeling a true affinity for the government contracting industry after so many years of immersion in it, he noted that his wife also had extensive executive leadership in the field and began to synthesize a fresh next step. "I wanted to stay active, I had a very good investment thesis, I wanted to combine my wife's and my backgrounds, and I wanted to do something with my colleagues who are interested in the defense industry," he explains. "Not only are we doing this, but we're doing it with many of the government contracting industry's leaders involved."

Though FedCap Advisors currently manages a single FedCap portfolio, Rick reports that it's only a matter of time before the forging of a second FedCap fund. He believes this endeavor may mark his last hurrah; whether or not this is true, it is safe to assume that the bliss that has driven his professional path to this point will continue to evolve.

"Don't get pigeonholed early in your career," Rick stresses to young entrepreneurs entering the business world today. "Your first jobs in the working world should be jobs where you're developing capabilities and skills. The first five or six years should be adding to your education and broadening your horizons; then you can decide which path you want to pursue and focus on."

Expanding on this, he recalls the advice his father gave him before leaving for college, which affirmed the importance of taking risks. "My father spoke with a trace of regret because he felt he hadn't taken enough risks in his life, and that resonated with me," he reports. "Whether for the worse or the better, I certainly haven't hesitated to enact change along my career path, and that has truly shaped the person I am."

Not only did risk-taking allow for greater reward, but it also allowed Rick to adjust his direction and momentum to remain true to his inner sense of calling. "I followed my bliss in terms of what I found interesting and challenging and exciting, and it was often with those things in mind that I acted, as opposed to focusing on building a solid foundation," he explains. "Forming the Windsor Group had felt so natural that I knew I had found my bliss, and that turned into something with lasting value. FedCap is the next stage of evolution of that bliss.

"And frankly," says Rick, "we're having a lot of fun."

Arthur Lafionatis

The Nonlinear Career Path

Most people go through childhood and young adulthood without a clearly defined passion to which they hope to dedicate their professional journey. Though this absence of a clear goal can be discouraging, it can also be a gift in disguise insofar as it encourages an individual to sample many different fields to find the one that's right for them. Other people, it seems, are born knowing what they want to be when they grow up and lead focused, determined, gratifying lives along the path to pursuing this singular goal.

Arthur Lafionatis, then, would represent the perfect synthesis of these two extremes, uniting the best of both worlds along the trajectory of his professional development. Now the managing partner and head of the Commercial Real Estate Transactions Group at Lerch, Early, & Brewer, a full-service commercial law firm headquartered in Bethesda, Maryland, he demonstrates how finding yourself doesn't have to mean limiting yourself, and how interests that fall outside the bounds of one's profession are not superfluous, but rather create a more textured and fascinating person overall.

Proud to have celebrated its 60th anniversary in 2010, Lerch, Early, & Brewer represents individuals, business owners, developers, contractors, and others throughout the D.C. metropolitan area and beyond. Through the orchestrated efforts of 33 partners and 17 associates, it specializes in ten diverse practice areas that include banking, real estate, land use, business, litigation, a labor & employment group, a community associations group, estate planning, divorces, and more. "We don't have all our eggs in one basket, and I think this speaks to a solid future for the firm," Art remarks.

Considering the firm's success and Art's current role in contributing toward and guiding it, one would think that he eats, sleeps, and breathes his role as managing partner. One might also think that this is the culmination of a very single-minded pursuit of excellence in the field, absorbing all time, resources, and hobbies. Art's story, however, diverges somewhat from these expectations.

Growing up in Massachusetts and New Hampshire, Art greatly admired and emulated one of his cousins throughout his childhood. This cousin was an attorney who later became an attorney general and then a state judge, and young Art wanted to be just like him, even though he hardly understood what it meant at the time. "For as long as I can remember, my plan was to get good grades, so that I could go to a good college, so that I could get into a good law school, so that I could become a lawyer," Art recalls.

He worked at a small town hardware store mixing paint to earn money early on and then put himself through college working at an ice cream shop, where he advanced over time from dishwasher to shift manager. His father had imparted the paramount importance of hard work, dedication, and integrity through his own example, so Art's determination and upward mobility came as no surprise. Then, the summer before he started law school, he was afforded the tremendous opportunity to work as a clerk with his cousin at the New Hampshire Supreme Court.

Art then attended law school at George Washington University, where he was instructed by a professor reputed to be among the national experts in governmental contracts. Several former students of this professor had just started their own firm, and they hired Art as a law clerk midway through his first year. They then asked him to stay on as an attorney upon graduating in 1980, and he served as a practicing lawyer for the following five years.

He enjoyed some exposure to government contracts and construction claim litigation during this time, but he was one of the only real estate transactional lawyers of the firm. In one notable example, the partner responsible for real estate from whom Art received much of his instruction actually got into an accident the night before a major closing, and because Art was the only other attorney with any kind of working knowledge on transactions, he found himself on a plane to Pittsburgh the next day to negotiate the multi-million dollar closing himself. Though he has since strayed from construction representation, Art remembers this period in his career as one that played a vital role in producing the lawyer he is today. "Because I have a better understanding of what's going on with the construction and development side of things, I am a better and more insightful real estate lawyer today, able to see both sides of the coin," he remarks.

Despite his proficiency in this capacity, Art realized that he was gravitating toward the transactional work he was doing and sought employment with a smaller real estate business boutique firm in downtown D.C. where he was able to learn the sophisticated nuance of his focus of choice. Hired on as senior associate, he then became partner two years later and served in that respect until the firm engaged in a relatively unsuccessful merger in 1993. Art was the last of his original colleagues to turn the lights off on the endeavor, and with that, he struck out to launch a law practice of his own.

"I bought a laptop and a multifunction fax printer, rented an executive suite, plugged it all in, and I was in business," Art remembers with a smile. Over the seven years of its life cycle, Art's firm fluctuated between one and seven employees until he was contacted in 2003 by an old friend from law school, Larry. Larry was employed with Lerch, Early, & Brewer, with whom Art had collaborated on a number of transactions over the years. The firm was looking to bring in a lateral real estate transactional partner in keeping with the vision of its strategic plan, and Art just so happened to fit the bill. He told Larry he wasn't looking to join a firm because he was happy with his own practice, but once he learned more about the strategic plan and the terms of the firm's governance and compensation structure, Art felt as though the opportunity had promise. "I began to entertain the notion that it was possible to go back into a larger firm environment without the headaches I had gotten in the past and with the benefits of collaborating with good lawyers that boasted a stellar reputation and company culture," Art explains. Thus, he accepted the position, bringing us to where he is today.

With such a natural career evolution, one would easily assume that Art never entertained other professional aspirations or pursuits. One would be surprised, then, to hear that he had many diverse interests, all of which he pursued freely, and many of which he still enjoys today. In college, for instance, he designed his own internship on Capitol Hill working for a senator from New Hampshire. "I still maintain that that job was the most fun I've ever had in my life," he reflects. "I didn't plan to go into politics, I just enjoyed the exposure to Washington." Subsequently, his choice to start his own law firm was made in part to allow him extra time to contribute to the writing and publication of a magazine focusing on affordable high-end audio products which he co-founded. In conjunction with a friend, Art kept the publication alive for four years. "The magazine didn't really take off, but my law practice did," he comments. "Still, I got to learn how a magazine is published and distributed, and I had a great time doing it."

Along a similar vein, Art has also cultivated a long-time love of computers that extends long before IBM even began manufacturing personal computers. "I played with the most archaic computers you can imagine in the late seventies," he recalls. "I've always liked gadgets, just trying to figure out how they work." Through this fascination, Art developed an impressive proficiency in the computerization of law firms, developing a litigation support database on an old Epson computer for the first firm he worked for. When he started his own firm, Art again employed these technologies, cutting costs and increasing productivity.

Despite this range of extraneous skills, Art came to Lerch, Early, & Brewer with a single finely-honed intention: that he would have a chance to build his real estate transactional practice within the context of this larger firm. "The idea of becoming managing partner wasn't even on my radar," he reflects. However, when the firm needed to upgrade its computer system and implement a document management system, he became a natural leader of the Technology Committee overseeing the projects. As a result, Art was asked to join the Management Committee a year and a half after joining the firm. The Committee is elected by consensus, and after serving a term of three years, he was ultimately rotated into the position of managing partner.

Art's career as an attorney, then, was not impeded by his decision to explore diverse areas of interest, but was rather enhanced by it. "People should know that I love being a lawyer, but that I have a lot of other interests as well," he says. "The audio magazine, computers, AV equipment and media, watching classic movies, the Greek Orthodox Church, photography… the list goes on and on. I'm not one of those people who won't know what I want to do when I retire because there are just too many things I enjoy doing."

These diverse interests and experiences may also factor into Art's unique ability to foster genuine and lasting relationships with his clients—a proclivity that is largely lacking in the legal field today. "My biggest successes are the several clients I have who've been with me for 20 or 25 years now," he remarks. "We've been through a lot of ups and downs together, but the relationship is still there and still strong." Whether this relational ability is derived from his parents, who were truly relationship people in all aspects of life, or whether it stems from his own ability to maintain an open, impassioned, and diverse perspective, Art's ability to connect with clients has allowed him to evolve into a better person and a better lawyer than he would have otherwise.

Through his ability to stay committed to a goal while also remaining open to other possibilities, preferences, and hobbies, Art reminds all young entrepreneurs entering the workforce today that we are each our own bosses. Whether we're employed for someone else or for ourselves, we ultimately have primary responsibility for ourselves and those reliant upon us. "At the end of the day, the only guarantee is what I can accomplish for my own clients and what I can accomplish for myself," he emphasizes. "Maintaining this sense of responsibility for yourself will help to guide you as you pursue your interests." The career path you take may not exactly be linear, but at least it will be honest, purposeful, and above all, a joy to experience.

Rosemary Tran Lauer

Daring to Care

Had Rosemary Tran Lauer learned to swim, her life would have been very different.

If she had ever been taught how, it is very likely that she would have leapt off the boat that day in April of 1975, with her three-year-old son and six-month-old daughter clutched in her arms. That day, she had been wandering the docks of Vietnam in search of her husband when a sailor, thinking she intended to come aboard his ship like so many other South Vietnamese at the brink of the fall of Saigon, whisked her son onto the deck. By the time she was able to run up the gangplank and recover the boy, throngs of refugees were already pressing in, desperate to flee the country and certain persecution in the wake of the Vietnam War. Violence broke out in the marina, and the ship was forced to disembark even as its captain was still trapped in the crowds on the dock.

With no food and only the clothes on their backs, Rosemary and her two children were taken to Guam, never to see her husband again. After ten days of misery at sea, they arrived at the island nation and settled in a tent city along with other refugees, struggling to survive and to piece together the sudden twist of fate that had ripped them from their home. "I've had a lot of challenges in my life, but I find they always happen for good reasons," Rosemary explains today.

Since she launched Devotion To Children, a volunteer-based organization dedicated to promoting quality early childcare for underprivileged families, these good reasons number in the hundreds and continue to multiply—and each one has a name, a face, and a future. Fueled by the passion and commitment of its idealistic volunteers, Devotion To Children raises funds to help pay for the care of children under six years of age while their parents go to work or attend school—an issue that hits very close to home for Rosemary.

By another twist of fate, Rosemary found herself in the right place at the right time in the tent city in Guam. She was able to appear in a news segment airing in the US, which led to her being sponsored to make the last leg of the journey to America, where she settled in Washington, D.C. The International Rescue Committee had organized a site for refugee housing in the city, and Rosemary was issued a small efficiency in which to make a new start. She hardly knew any English at all, but she knew she had to provide for her children. Unable to afford childcare, she asked a neighboring family to watch over her son and daughter as she struck out in search of employment.

When Rosemary was approached by the owner of the Arabian restaurant next door and offered a job as a waitress, she didn't hesitate. "My survival instinct is quite strong," she says. "I couldn't pronounce any English words, but I could read the numbers on the menu. Customers could point to the number, and I could then report that to the kitchen. I memorized every item number, and I did a lot of smiling."

The income helped, but at such a low wage, Rosemary knew she needed something more. In no time she found herself working three jobs, toiling around the clock to provide for her children, whom she rarely saw. Eventually, however, her working conditions turned dangerous, and she knew it was time to try a different approach. With that, she went on welfare and, with the help of government education aid for refugees, enrolled in cosmetology school.

"Everything I do, with the grace of God, I do with all my heart," says Rosemary. This exceptional investment of true heart and soul shone in the uncommon elegance with which she tended her clients. One such client was quick to admire her unparalleled skill and offered to go into business with Rosemary, proposing to purchase the salon herself and to split the profits with the talented beautician while she ran the business.

With that, a true entrepreneur was born, and in just several short years, Rosemary's salon was already enjoying more success than others who had been in the business for twenty years. A dispute with her business partner, however, later compelled her to leave the establishment to start up another salon, which she operated for 17 very successful years.

While successful, these years were not without their trials. The driven businesswoman married a man with two children from a previous marriage, and after they had three more, Rosemary found herself raising all seven while balancing the demands of the salon. When the pair later divorced and she was left with no child support or alimony, life grew more demanding still, yet she remained as committed and headstrong as ever, driven toward success by an inner fire that would never flicker. "I started all over again, selling my old salon and then starting a new one that was over double in size, with several dozen employees," Rosemary recalls.

As she pursued success as a business owner, she also used this persistent inner fire to found Devotion To Children in 1994, and since that day, Rosemary and her team have worked tirelessly to address a need that truly lies at the root of our society's well being. "We talk about breaking the cycle of poverty, but sometimes we miss the mark because we're not focusing on the fact that children are the future," she points out. "For every one dollar we invest in a child now, we save 18 dollars down the road by putting that child on a path that is healthy and productive. If we don't help these children early on in their most formative years, we're not only hurting each child, but also ourselves and the whole of society."

Throughout the six years of single motherhood that followed her divorce, Rosemary's efforts with Devotion To Children aimed to fill the certain void in society that she, herself, was struggling through. Then, in 1999, she met her current husband, Bill Lauer, through her efforts with Devotion To Children and decided to sell her successful salon business to finally have more time with her family.

As fate would have it, she was diagnosed with breast cancer 2001, yet ever the survivor, she triumphed over the disease with characteristic vigor. At that point, she decided to start over yet again, but this time in an entirely different field—real estate. "Because of my experience as a business owner, commercial real estate came very naturally to me, even though it is a heavily male-dominated field," she explains. "As an Asian American woman in that environment, my clients really like me."

One can be certain these clients have rarely met anyone who works as hard or with as much spirit as Rosemary does, and it is with this same spirit that she continues the work of Devotion To Children today. Affordable, quality childcare is nearly impossible to find in the DC metro area, with waiting lists for such organizations extending several hundred names long. This is particularly troubling in light of research indicating that the first three years of a child's life are the most important in that the fundamental processes of life are developing at their most rapid pace.

Recognizing the vital importance of this early intellectual stimulation, interaction, and support, Devotion To Children directs its services at assisting children under the age of six, as formal schooling helps to alleviate the burden of care after that point. "So many families can barely survive or afford food, let alone books," says Rosemary, all too familiar with the stark reality of that fact. "In a perfect world, men and women should be able to give their all in the workplace, knowing that their children are being cared for by nurturing professionals. Devotion To Children is committed to bringing us a little closer to that perfect world. That's my dream."

This is not only Rosemary's dream, but also the passion of Devotion To Children's committed team of eight board members and 42 young volunteers, who clock in countless hours on top of their regular jobs to ensure that the initiative remains successful. Thanks to their efforts, the organization's fundraising success continues to escalate by 25 percent annually despite the recession. Sponsors rest assured knowing that every penny of their donations goes directly to funding the cause, which impacts hundreds of lives each year through the support of day-care facilities, extended childcare programs, Head Start libraries, and scholarships for children under six.

What is perhaps most striking about Rosemary's character is not merely the magnitude of her impact in the wake of incredible adversity, but more so the fact that she has been able to maintain an openness and innocence of spirit that is so often decimated by the trials of modern society. It's as if she chose to treat her hardships not as weights, but as balloons, elevating her to loftier goals and bigger dreams. "I've always been very naïve and trusting, so if someone criticizes me, I believe that they're telling me the truth and I don't disregard it," she explains. "If it's something I can't change about myself, then I accept it. If it's something I can change, I change it. This allows me to be very accepting of reality, without the clouding that comes when people take criticism too personally. I accept reality as it is, pairing this with a fierce determination to always do better, and I believe that the 'ideal world' people so often refer to should be treated as a viable objective to strive for."

What if every person in America lived their lives with the kind of passion that inundates Rosemary's story? It is a passion born not only in perseverance, but also in a deeply rooted, genuine belief in humanity's ability to transcend the adversity that falls in its path. "When we hear about problems today, so many people will just say that they don't care," Rosemary reflects. "Something I am still trying to understand is how to instill in people the desire to change things, because these things affect everyone."

Indeed, Americans today so often assume an attitude of powerlessness in the face of the larger social issues that plague our nation. Perhaps it is that the ills of our society seem so monumental that one person couldn't possibly make a difference, so why try?

"We *have* to care," insists one person—a small, first generation Vietnamese immigrant woman without a college education, who came to this country with nothing, but who believed in something. Now this woman works tirelessly to give back to the community that helped her to attain the grace and success of her full potential, and through Devotion To Children, this cycle of mutual betterment promises to extend far into the future.

Chris Lessard

A Blueprint for Success

"Every horrible thing turned out to be a good thing," says Chris Lessard, as his mind traces back over the events of his life and connects the dots. When he first entered the architectural industry at age 27, his world seemed as though it was falling apart. Recently divorced with a young child and not a clue as to how to navigate such terrain, he recalls the hopelessness that permeated his perception. "Then I saw an ad in the Washington Post for a hotshot designer for a group based out of Philadelphia," he recalls. "I went in to interview, and they asked me to run their D.C. office." Now the CEO of Lessard Design Inc. and the designer of several hundred thousand units and counting, Chris's legacy is a testament to perseverance and faith, hard work and heart.

"As an architect, you have a chance to engender real buildings that encapsulate someone's experience, like the joy of moving to a new place," he marvels. "This company has advanced so far beyond the buildings themselves. We're about the socialization of the buildings—the connectivity, the experience, the impact."

Of course, it was not all fun and games from the moment he decided to answer the ad in the paper. Though he did some research before accepting the position, he remained wholly surprised by the conditions he confronted when he showed up for his first day of work. Indeed, the office was minimal and the staff difficult. "I thought I had just screwed up big time," he remembers. "I thought my career was over!"

What's more, Chris had taken a pay cut to accept his new position, which worsened that initial blow. "When it comes to knowledge versus money, I always opt for knowledge," he explains. "Let money take care of itself. I took that pay cut because I reasoned that I would not have incentives otherwise. I didn't know it would work out, but hey, I was divorced and could take those chances." Though it is widely understood that great rewards often require great risk, life's responsibilities often preclude the possibility of taking these risks. From the ashes of Chris's despair, however, came the opportunity to take one such risk. "In the end, it never turned out to be a pay cut," he says. "Rather, it turned out to double my pay, and with the learned knowledge added to that, the experience has been immeasurable."

Like its founder, Lessard Design is multi-faceted and textured. Though Chris considers himself an architect first and foremost, the various groups housed under the Lessard Group name are investments that lend long-term stability to his portfolio. One such offshoot, Lessard Commercial, deals with retail, office, and auto dealership space, while another, Lessard Private Limited, lends an international presence to the firm that assists in segregating liability and establishing separate internal business units. Still another component, Metropolitan Development, specializes in apartment construction, while various other sub-groups tend to leasing and asset management, one-off real estate deals, and the like.

Lessard Design was first launched as CJ Lessard Architects and Land Planners in 1986 after Chris left his position running a branch division for The Martin Architectural Group, a firm based out of Philadelphia. He had served in that capacity for four years, working 80-hour weeks doing the designs himself and essentially cultivating the identity of the firm. Though he had the opportunity to venture out on his own on several occasions during that interval, he held out until the time was right, rendering the transition fairly easy and allowing him to earn a profit after the very first month.

Despite this smooth and seamless progression, Chris found himself at another crossroads with the advent of his second divorce. Following the guidance of an attorney, he quit CJ Lessard Architects and borrowed $100,000 from friends to launch Lessard Architecture and Land Planners, offering up his own architectural services as collateral. "Society trains you to think linearly, but that's detrimental," Chris reflects, drawing upon the strategies of his own trade and applying them to the strategy of life. "You have to think outside the box. Many rules prevent you from getting ahead, so you have to analyze them and push back where appropriate. Suppose you need money to accomplish what you want to accomplish? This is not insurmountable. Find opportunities somehow by rearranging the order of what you do."

One particularly compelling aspect of Chris's approach is his ability to harness and abate the element of risk through the tools of self-assurance and attitude. "The thing is that if you believe in yourself, you've automatically eliminated a lot of the perceived risk," he points out. "This doesn't mean it will always work out, but if you're engaged and flexible enough, you'll bounce around and get the right answer eventually."

Today, the Lessard companies are 70 employees strong with a management group of four. The efforts of this team are supplemented by a number of contractors hired to oversee the enterprise's actual projects. Though the majority of its work occurs in the U.S., it also serves markets in India and Saudi Arabia in an effort to reduce cost basis by increasing their market share after the recent economic downturn.

Chris's career is perhaps most directly influenced by his father, who was a homebuilder. After graduating early from Virginia Tech, Chris entered the industry as well, supervising his father's housing construction in Richmond. "Most people don't realize that homebuilding is cash flow management," he reflects. After analyzing the business's profitability, he recommended that they close up shop—a fortuitous suggestion in light of the fact that his father was diagnosed with cancer six months later and passed away soon thereafter. "I was able to get that business shut down and to get into architecture, and although I didn't continue directly in that industry, I still use the knowledge it imparted everyday," he says. "I'm able to understand not only the business of my client base, but also the numbers of the Washington market."

It is precisely this understanding that sets Chris and his team apart from their peers, identifying Lessard Design as a key shaper and assessor of value in an industry that is so often unpredictable. "My experience out of school allowed me to really understand the value of things—not just the process of planning or architecture, but the logic and reasoning behind it, as well as the financial aspects," says Chris. "To this day, when people come to me looking for guidance, we not only achieve their goal, but we explain how and why." Therein lies the uniqueness of Lessard Design.

The integrity of the group's expertise is matched, honed, and balanced by the integrity of its character, which is coordinated by a core value system—a trait Chris lists as number one in importance. "There are too many decisions in life, and you cannot focus on the hard ones unless you have a basis for properly and effectively addressing the smaller ones," he illustrates. "You have to have core guidance to leave you time to handle the hard complications your life will undoubtedly throw you at some points." In a world where so many people strive to please everybody, Chris emphasizes the importance of having the guts to commit to a set of values, as there will always be someone who thinks these values are wrong. "Sometimes you have to take chances, and it's hard to know if you're right. The only thing that will give you courage is your core value system," he reflects.

This value system, combined with Chris's willingness to take big risks, results in a decision making style that is at once freeing and profitable. Reflecting on people who dedicate large amounts of time trying to make the "right" decision, he points out the illogicality of such an approach. "With the time they spend doing that, I make ten decisions. Suppose two of them are the wrong decisions. Still, it puts you much further ahead than the other strategy does." As well, he points out that, if a decision is identified as the "wrong" thing, one can simply turn around and make it right, which speaks to the protean character of life and again harkens back to the notion that one is not bound to a linear path to success.

According to this ideology, success is also lent through perception and an acute awareness of the term's more nuanced mechanics. "So much of success is about helping everyone feel a part of it," Chris says. "When confronted with a problem, you must find a solution that makes everyone look good. If you can get there, you'll win. If you can't, you'll lose. People have their own sets of issues, needs, and requirements. Helping everyone to feel like a winner will, in turn, allow you to win."

This ties in strongly with Chris's leadership philosophy, which places a strong emphasis on the prominence of passion and goals in the workplace and in life. Identifying the reality that most people fail to firm up their goals into a concrete and objectively measurable outcome, he strives to structure the good intentions of his employees into notions that are firmly sketched in outline, detail, and deadline. "That is truly the key for people coming out of school—to have concrete goals," he emphasizes. Along a similar vein, Chris presses the importance of lofty goals—what he terms "multiplier" goals because their strict parameters engender innovative and out-of-the-box solutions. "Some of my goals force us to figure out new ways to do things," he acknowledges. "By being unwavering in our sights and pressing for new solutions, we are challenging our company to evolve."

Chris not only embraces these elements of risk and creativity in his professional life, but in his personal life as well. "The more theater you put in your life, the more you can really impart life lessons to those in it," he reveals. Whether it's plotting an elaborate date for his wife or staging an incredible coming-of-age ceremony for his son, he invests an insurmountable amount of time and energy into stretching the boundaries of reality and thereby creating new realities—realities that are rich with meaning and reflection, self-awareness and possibility. "Success leaves trails," says Chris, quoting the compelling life coach, Tony Robbins. Just as Chris himself has charted and followed the route to success as demonstrated by others, so can today's young entrepreneurs chart and follow the route to success as demonstrated by him.

Dick Lombardo

The Critical Path

The critical path. The shortest route from beginning to end, and among the most fascinating aspects of Dick Lombardo's workday. As the President and CEO of Harkins Builders, a leader in the Mid-Atlantic region's construction management industry, he is the first to affirm that a project is never about one person. Rather, it's about using collaborative, analytical discourse to map out a critical path that will bring their clients an impeccable end result.

To best determine what this critical path is, Harkins Builders fosters a think-tank-like environment in which a project's entire team gathers, along with several additional voices with relevant experience. In this meeting, the team lays out the project's schedule and then completely tears it apart, rearranging it and shaving months off the timeline through the input of seasoned expertise and fresh perspectives alike. "Putting together a schedule in this manner for a large project can be exceedingly challenging in that you can have thousands of activities to sequence, coordinate, and time," Dick explains. "But in that challenge lies tremendous opportunity, and I love the discussion and analysis that goes into maximizing that opportunity."

Dick's collaborative leadership style falls flush with Harkins's long tradition of fostering independence and agency within its workforce—an approach that dates back to its foundation in 1965 by Thomas P. Harkins himself. Mr. Harkins had been President of Carl M. Freeman Associates, a large residential multi-family and single-family developer, when he decided to strike out on his own as a builder developer. A number of other developers, however, sought his services to build for them, setting the tone for the company's identity as a contractor.

Tom was a kind and thoughtful man of deep integrity, and he founded Harkins upon a belief in the human spirit's capacity to think, grow, and assume leadership. It was exactly the kind of environment Dick needed when he first approached the company in 1975. Having graduated in 1970 from what was then Loyola College in Baltimore, he married the following year and got a construction job as an assistant superintendent building apartments in Annapolis. After several years, Dick decided to go into business with a colleague to form their own general contracting company, which survived for several years doing smaller projects.

When the real estate recession hit in 1975, Dick's fledgling company hadn't picked up enough momentum to weather the storm, and he soon found himself unable to pay the bills and to support his two young sons. That's when he went in to interview at Harkins, meeting with Jim Humphrey, who was acting as President at the time.

In the interview, Jim asked Dick what his long-term plans were, to which Dick responded with unflinching honesty that he intended to work for Harkins for a year or so and then pursue his entrepreneurial dreams by striking out on his own again.

"Why would you expect me to hire you for a year so you can go out and compete with me?" Jim asked.

"Because in that year I'll be the best employee you've got," Dick affirmed.

Whether it was Jim's belief in the young man sitting across from him or in the company itself, he extended an offer of employment to Dick, and what was supposed to be a one-year tenure turned into a lasting and compelling relationship that has run thirty-five years and counting.

Originally hired as an assistant estimator, Dick hit the ground running, working on much larger projects than he'd ever worked on before from the very outset. A year later, he moved out into the field where he worked as a project manager. In 1981, he assumed responsibility for the firm's first design-build project, wherein the city of Baltimore was advertising for someone to facilitate the construction of an elderly housing site. Dick selected the property, designed the project, and won the contract to develop the nine-story apartment building. He became a division manager in 1987.

That same year, Dick was approached by a builder developer company that offered him a position with a pay increase sizable enough that he could not, in good conscience, turn it down. "I had a young family at the time, and I felt like I owed it to them to take that opportunity," he reflects now. When he notified the Harkins leadership team of his intention, they were distraught to lose him, but Mr. Harkins didn't seem concerned. He let Dick know that, if he ever wanted his old job back, he need do nothing more than walk into the office and sit down at his desk again, bidding Dick adieu with characteristic warmth.

Dick's sign-on bonus was to be paid upon six months of employment at the new firm, but after five months and three weeks, he found himself strolling through the Harkins doors once more, taking a seat in that familiar chair and picking up where he left off. "The other company was the exact opposite of where I had come from," says Dick. "All the power rested with one person, and the people surrounding that person were not expected to think. My only role there was to carry out orders, and it just really wasn't for me." Soon thereafter, he was promoted to VP of Harkins.

When Mr. Harkins passed away in 1993, Blase Cooke, who had been acting as President and CEO, assumed ownership of the company. Blase had developed strong leadership skills under Mr. Harkins, and the company continued to flourish with his guidance. In 2001, he decided to sell a majority of its stock to the employees, forming an Employee Stock Option Plan (ESOP) that would truly marry the Harkins team to the fruits of its labor by promoting an engaged, self-interested workforce. When Blase later passed away in 2007 after a heroic battle with cancer, Dick, who was acting as Executive Vice President and COO at the time, became President and CEO.

Today, after a long story of steadily unfolding success, Harkins has reached a net worth of $20 million, with 65 percent of its stock held through its ESOP and the remaining 35 percent held by its executives. "Everyone has a stake in the game, and this changes how people think and act," Dick reports. As such, Harkins's 200-employee workforce succeeded in generating around $225 million in revenues last year.

This success came even despite the conditions of the last several years, which have been horrific for the construction industry. Indeed, Harkins has remained extraordinarily profitable while suffering only minor reductions in volume, indicating a level of health and vitality that is practically unheard of amongst similar organizations. "Never have we worked harder to find the work we have, and the market is far more competitive than it's ever been, but we do go out there and find success," Dick reports. To supplement the firm's renown as a multifamily builder, Harkins has also developed a solid standing with the Army Corp of Engineers, the Navy, and the Air Force. Though his proudest accomplishment will always be his three children, Dick's hand in maintaining and expanding the company's volume through innovative partnerships and firm commitment amidst tough conditions cannot be overlooked.

What has enabled Harkins to survive and thrive despite several economic downturns, and what has captivated the fidelity of talented and driven individuals like Dick and his predecessors for over forty years?

Dick himself maintains that it is the culture of intellectualism, agency, and support that first drew him to the company, and one would be hard-pressed to disagree. "Harkins created an environment where you are both allowed and expected to take on as much as you can and to make decisions," he explains. "Nobody ever got in trouble here for making a mistake. This company has always been big on encouraging people to really use their brains, to lead, and to take risks."

So unique from other organizations where hierarchy, seniority, and uniformity are more the norm, Harkins's focus on collaboration and support truly render it greater than the sum of its parts. "When two or more brains work together, there's teamwork," Dick points out. "There's a lot more productivity, and it's my job to promote and participate in that culture and process."

In advising young entrepreneurs entering the workforce today, Dick stresses the importance of being a sponge. "Work hard, ask questions, and learn as much as you can," he urges. "Always be focused on your next objective." Perhaps his most unique piece of advice, however, is the stripping of ego from mission that is so inherent in finding the critical path of a project, allowing one to focus entirely on the outcome and on the needs of the client rather than on their own personal success. "As my father always said, it's never about you," Dick explains. "It's about an objective, a goal, or whatever is at hand. If you can take yourself out of it and keep your focus on your objective, you'll be successful."

Adhering to this mantra all his life, it's no wonder that Dick found a perfect professional match in Harkins Builders, guided by its mission-driven attitude and its commitment to fostering independent thought. With the help of this mentality, the business currently boasts an average employee tenure of 15 years, even though they're hiring young people all the time. "I've been with the company 35 years, and our executives and project managers have been with the company an average of more than 20 years," Dick says. Though the national average is trending toward much more splintered career paths in today's workforce, Harkins once again defies the norms. "We're a company that cares about its employees and community, that gives opportunities, that expects performance, and that rewards it," he affirms. Through its appeal to talent both young and old, Harkins is able to deliver consistently, bringing to the industry table a service that is as impressive as it is effective, and whose expertise prevents problems just as readily as it solves them.

Harry Martens III

Defying the New Normal

Henry Ford of Ford Motor Company first knocked on L.P. Steuart's door in the early nineteen hundreds—a knock that would reverberate through the Steuart/Martens family for a hundred years to come and in ways the young boy could never have imagined at the time.

"I'd like your help selling my machine around this area," Mr. Ford told the young man. L.P., who had dropped out of school in the eighth grade along with his brother to support the family, had started a hauling business serving downtown Washington, D.C. With a second-hand cart hooked up to an old mule, the boys would deliver coal in the winter and ice blocks in the summer. Having come to know and serve the folks of the region, their renown and expertise was ideal for Mr. Ford's lofty objective: to bring the car industry to the nation's capital.

"My grandfather used to tell us that selling the cars was only half the battle," remarks Harry Martens III, now the President of Martens

Cars of Washington Inc. a century later. "The other half was actually teaching the buyers how to drive. In those days, nobody drove. It was a brand new undertaking, and that's how our business started."

Since that first and fateful knock on the door, the business grew over time as more car manufacturers took root in the area. As the numerous small manufacturers began to consolidate, the company acquired a DeSoto distributorship, selling DeSoto cars along the East Coast. Harry's grandfather also branched into the Chrysler arena, at one point in possession of eight Chrysler dealerships in the Washington area, which marked the enterprise's most robust period.

Harry's father met Mr. Steuart's daughter when he was released from the Army after serving in World War II, and he fit seamlessly into the gears of the business. Despite the addition of a family member into the management structure, however, "Mr. L.P." couldn't help but feel that his company seemed less and less like a family business the greater it grew. "My grandfather always ran this as a family business and with a corresponding set of values," Harry reflects. "He treated his employees and customers in accordance with those values, which became more challenging as the business expanded and the atmosphere became less personal."

Thus, when he realized he no longer knew all the names of his customers, his employees, and their families, Harry's grandfather and father decided it was time to pare the business back. "As you get big, you get impersonal," Harry acknowledges. "You lose the family element that makes the business so unique and worthwhile. Thus, through an evolution influenced both internally and by external factors, we eventually whittled back down to one primary location with two brands—Volvo and Volkswagen."

Harry's grandfather, whom he affectionately refers to as "Pop-Pop", worked until the day he died when, at the age of 86, he had a heart attack. "Nobody was going to retire him," Harry smiles now, remembering the man's unparalleled work ethic and heartfelt commitment.

Harry's father later passed away in 2004, and Harry now views the continuation of his patriarch's legacy as the North Star that guides his professional journey.

"Maintaining the family values that my father and grandfather honored so deeply is our absolute top priority here," he says. "We've had many opportunities to buy other franchises and dealerships, some of which were quite appealing. But when it came down to it, we thought about what our grandfather would want us to do. Indeed, his influence continues to be our guiding principle today." This ideology is encapsulated in the business's mission statement, which Harry penned back in the seventies. "Our goal is to be the best car dealership in the Washington, D.C. area," Harry proclaims. "Not the biggest, but the best."

Long before he began his journey with Martens Cars, Harry's first job was delivering Washington Posts in the morning, earning extra money because he yearned for some measure of independence. For several years, the young boy would rise every morning at 4:30 come two feet of snow or early morning thunderstorms, riding up to each house and carefully placing the paper in its carriage.

The summer he turned 14, Harry's father told him he would work in the parts department at his store on P Street. Even now, he remembers the words of wisdom his Dad delivered the night before his first day of work. "I'm going to tell you exactly what I expect of you," Harry senior had said. "I expect you to be down there a half hour before anybody else arrives, and I expect you to leave a half hour after everybody else leaves. I expect you to work three times harder than anybody else because you're the boss's son, and everybody's eyes are going to be on you."

Replicating this effective dose of tough love, Mr. Martens also obliged his son to find his own way to work, which involved biking to the bus stop and then switching bus routes each morning and each evening. "I can vaguely remember my father driving past me and waving," Harry recalls, reflecting on the convoluted commute.

Still, not even the arduous journey to and from work could hinder the quick and natural affinity Harry felt for the job, and he returned the following summer to work in the store's service department. The summer after that, he returned as a service advisor. "I basically did all the jobs in the dealership, which is the best way to learn," Harry affirms.

As a young man, Harry never explicitly sat back to consider what he wanted to do with his life—which goals he wanted to pursue, or what he wanted to be. Rather, fulfilling the family legacy seemed to be almost as innate as breathing, and as natural as a heartbeat. "I don't know that it was conscious," he examines. "It was just there. It was an unspoken thing."

After high school, Harry attended Brown University—a decision he attributes to his grandfather. Each time he would visit his grandfather as a child, the old man would ask how his grades were. "He didn't have a formal education, and it was perhaps for that exact reason that he could truly recognize how valuable it was," Harry surmises. "Drilling this importance into us in this manner gave me a true determination to do well in school and to achieve some good."

After graduating from Brown with a degree in economics and serving a tour in the Navy, Harry returned home and slipped naturally into a new role as the marketing manager for Volvo Cars of America. He served in that capacity for a year, helping to find new dealers for Volvo in the region extending from Pennsylvania to Florida, until his father notified him that he was needed at the family Volvo store. "Again, I didn't ask questions," Harry recalls. "I reported for work on January 2nd, 1973."

Having spent his high school summers working the back end of the business, which was heavily focused in parts and service, he was more than well versed in the value of genuine and heartfelt customer care. "My grandfather had always stressed that, if we really took care of our customers in the service end of the business, they would trust us and come back to buy their new cars from us in the future," he recalls. When he started in 1973, however, he found himself operating the sales end of the business for the first time. "I had to learn from the ground up at that point, but it was great," he remarks.

Assuming more responsibility over time and coming to master every detail, large and small, of the business, Harry has since dedicated his professional life to Martens Cars. This is not to suggest, however, that he did not stop to question the path his life had so naturally assumed. In 1980, he realized it was time to confront that question. "I hit a wall and asked myself for the first time if the car business was really what I wanted to do with my life," he recalls. "I realized I could keep doing it, or I could stop and try something new, and I wanted to try something on my own that I was responsible for without the support of the whole company."

As fate would have it, he seized the opportunity and decided, after much groundwork, to subdivide the 200-acre farm that had belonged to his grandfather into 55 lots and launch a real estate development company. Partnering with a close friend and using their joint expertise in construction, design, marketing, and finance, Martens Edwards Development Company was born. "At one point we had a townhouse project in Fairfax County, another in Frederick, and four or five other projects going at once, and I absolutely loved it," Harry recalls. "I loved starting with nothing but raw ground, creating something, and then stepping back to see what we had done."

Like so many developing companies during that time, Martens Edwards met an untimely but respectable end in the real estate depression of the early 1990s, yet Harry was able to optimize the hardship by drawing invaluable leadership skills that assist him today at the helm of Martens Cars. "That experience really reinforced the idea that what goes up must come down, so you better be ready for it by planning ahead to find a way through it," he points out. "Businesses and young people who haven't gone through a recession and learned this yet will find this a harder lesson to learn than most."

Such a skill has been exceptionally advantageous in the past several years, as Martens Cars has ridden the wave of the recent recession with a measure of grace that suggests the enterprise will persevere for years to come. Yet the company's surfing ability can hardly take credit for the bulk of its staying power. Rather, that honor goes to the enduring atmosphere of family values that the business continues to live, breathe, and impart. "People are always talking about the "new normal"—the change in philosophy and ethics that has been ushered into society along with our new technologies and ways of life—but I prefer to stay committed to old fashioned values like integrity, responsibility, and work ethic," Harry stresses.

Indeed, Martens Cars was first born into the kind of world where someone could buy a $3 million piece of property through the binding trust and mutual respect garnered through a simple handshake. It didn't take contracts, signatures, or written agreements to inspire both parties to abide by an agreement as it does so often in today's society. "There are some rare people who you can still shake hands with and know their word is their bond," Harry reflects, "and it's impossible to overemphasize the sacredness of that." Thus, in a world where the status quo leaves much to be desired, Martens Cars remains committed to infusing this "new normal" with the timeless values that enable us to have faith in the human relationship, whether professional, personal, or one in the same.

Michael McDevitt

Affecting the Trends

"In recent years," Michael McDevitt reports, "we have watched the trending of obesity rise from less than 50 to well over 65 percent in America, and it seems as though we're beginning to export this unhealthy lifestyle and diet worldwide." As the CEO of Medifast, Inc., among the most competitive and comprehensive weight loss programs on the market today, Michael uses these startling statistics not only to measure the current climate, but also to outline a dream for tomorrow. "Medifast's goal is to reverse that trend," he affirms.

Medifast was first launched in 1980. The company developed a line of medically formulated meal replacements to help individuals lose weight, and these were sold to physicians. Reimbursable at the time, the doctors would then sell the meals to their patients and coach them on successful weight loss.

The company was quite successful until 1996, amassing an almost $50 million wholesale business until the insurance industry changed the rules of the game and no longer reimbursed patients for the product. The sales of the Medifast clinically-proven meal replacements almost plummeted from an estimated $50 million to zero overnight, and it was clear that the physician-as-middleman business model was no longer viable.

The company struggled to redefine itself from 1996 through 2001, investing in additional meal replacement product lines and testing the waters to try and find something that worked. At the end of this experimentation phase, one thing had become clear: that the new Medifast should take its program directly to the consumers, and that the weight loss product they were offering was only half the equation. "In the weight loss industry, as it is with so many industries, people too often get caught up in focusing on the product," Michael explains. "Without the added refinement of education and behavior modification, there is no long-term success."

When he first joined the company in 2002, it had set its sights on a new strategy—one that was direct, holistic, and empowering. "What we wanted to do with Medifast was to create a support system that would allow consumers to buy the product directly from the company," he explains. "The company would then support them as they used the product in their homes." In this new business model, they planned to sell the meal and service package through the Internet and through a contact center. The meals would be shipped to the door of the customers, who could then receive support via an online toolkit or by calling the contact center. Slowly but surely, Medifast began to see the light at the end of the tunnel, and their sales grew to $5 to $12 million annually between 2001 and 2002.

Michael and the Medifast team began to notice, however, that the scope of their impact didn't have to stop there. "Consumers kept calling to ask what more they could do," Michael remembers. "They would say how much they loved what we were doing and how much it was helping them, and they would ask how they could help their friends and family find the same success." At first, Medifast considered instituting a referral program. "We ended up putting that concept on steroids to embrace the concept of direct selling," Michael continues. "Our customers were so passionate that it only made sense to channel this passion, training them to be living, breathing proof and advocates of the product... proof their family and friends could really believe in."

Called the Take Shape for Life program, this initiative was launched in 2003 in tandem with the Direct Response program, in which customers could literally join the business through the Internet. The enterprise took off immediately, doing $6 to $12 million in sales within two years. "The irony about a weight loss and nutrition program is that, if it doesn't work, you have short-term success and then long-term failure," Michael explains. "On the other hand, if it works, the business grows."

One can only surmise, then, that Medifast works. A huge contributor to the company's success, and what sets it apart from its competitors, has been the constant interaction it fosters with its customer base, allowing Michael and his team to respond and adapt quickly to the suggestions and demands of consumers. "We're lucky to have direct contact with our consumers," Michael points out. "When you sell only through a middleman like a retail location, you lose touch with your consumers. You only know the relationship with the stores. We decided to take our product directly to the consumers, and we've been listening to them ever since, finding new ways to improve our company through their comments and advice."

True to form, Medifast kept listening, and they heard their client base express an interest in a higher level of accountability. "Our coaching system and tools were great, but they were saying they wanted more, so we set about delivering that," says Michael. Thus, in 2005, the company launched its brick-and-mortar weight control centers, where customers could go and receive one-on-one training from licensed professionals that coached them through various weight loss phases. "At this point, we're the only business I'm aware of that's selling the same product at the same price through three different support channels all focused on different types of consumers and their varying needs," Michael affirms.

Whether you want complete autonomy over your weight loss routine, the coaching of a successful friend or family member, or the gold standard and support of a physical one-on-one licensed professional, Medifast truly has something for everyone. And in driving their customers to success, the company has found unprecedented success itself. All three business models grew at rates over 30 percent in 2010, and the company as a whole closed at a staggering $257 million in sales.

Despite its breadth of service offerings, Medifast is all about keeping things simple. "Considering the modern American lifestyle and how busy our customers are these days, convenience and simplicity is everything," says Michael. "Research shows that, by eating five Medifast meals per day plus one regular meal, you lose between two and five pounds a week, and that's twice what other commercial weight loss companies can claim."

Though fortuitous and fitting, one might not guess from Michael's background that he would wind up the CEO of a company like Medifast. In fact, he graduated with a finance and computer information systems degree from James Madison University in 2000 and assumed employment at the Blackstone Group, an investment bank in New York City, where he lived the Wall Street life. "Even as a kid, I was engulfed—not in the money side of finance, but in the game that it was," Michael remembers. "From a young age, I loved picking up the paper and following the trends in the stock market. How could I figure out what would drive things up or down?" The more time he spent in the finance and investment world, however, the more he came to realize that it was primarily about helping a small group of people. Michael discovered that he not only wanted to understand and capitalize on trends, but also to affect and change them, reaching a much larger demographic of individuals and changing as many lives as he could.

When he came across the opportunity to join Medifast, Michael's interest was immediately piqued. Trading at 12 cents a share on the over-the-counter market, the struggling company struck a chord in his entrepreneurial spirit and resonated with his upbringing, which had heavily revolved around a philosophy of exercise and nutrition. His mother would prepare a balanced and nutritional dinner every night while he was growing up, and it was only later in life that Michael became aware that 90 percent of Americans aren't raised in that kind of environment, opting instead for fast or junk food. "Obesity is a tremendous problem in our nation today, and I wanted to be part of something that would reverse that trend," he explains. "It's heavily impacting the economy, health care, and job effectiveness. Medifast gave me the opportunity to come in on the ground floor in an industry that I love and just make an amazing difference."

The company had about 25 employees when he started, and not much else. "We were a clean sheet of paper," he remembers. "We had to write the story of how we were going to do this. We had to take our passion and make the tracks in the snow ourselves, and this combination of subject matter and challenge was a dream come true for me." Michael came on board as the Vice President of Finance, but because the leadership team was so small, everyone had a say in everything that went on. From there, he transitioned into the role of President, and then to CEO in 2007.

Among the most fascinating aspects of Michael's leadership is perhaps his ability to usher his metric-minded system of measurement and analysis into the fabric of the business's operation, organizing the more human and relationship aspects of leadership into a framework that is consistent and effective. "I think that getting an accounting degree is one of the best ways to learn how a business works," he says. "It's a great knowledge base, and you can then look at other departments, like I did when I came to Medifast. There's a lot of opportunity for those armed with that knowledge to connect the dots."

In advising young entrepreneurs entering the business world today, Michael also encourages one to welcome assistance and embrace wisdom from others when tackling an unknown task, citing his refusal to ask for help as a young CEO to be his biggest fault. "I wanted to prove to people that I could do it, but what I realize now is that I wasn't expected to now everything right off the bat," he reports. "There is a rich trove of experience surrounding you, so use that experience to empower yourself. Life is most lived in communication. You're only as alive as your ability to communicate with other individuals."

With this in mind, it is surprising to learn that Michael is hard-wired as an introvert and has spent the past year focusing on improving his self-awareness. "In order to be a leader of others, you must first be truly aware of yourself, how you tick, and how you react to things," he points out. "Bettering yourself is a constant process, and the more you grow, the more you can help others."

Introverted, yet quick to expound the merits of reaching out and communicating with others. Metric-driven, yet keenly in touch with the notion that business and success is all about human relationships. And, of course, a literal trendsetter. How do such characteristics coexist within the same man? "I love the extremes in life," Michael explains. "I love walking outside the common path and living outside the lines. It's not for shock value, it's to see how far we can stretch something to make it the best it can be. This is just how I am, and it's what drove me to where I am today."

And where is that, exactly? 250 thousand people had life altering experiences with Medifast's products last year, and, as many would argue, this is just the beginning.

Dr. Alan Merten

The Amplification of Impact

Upon taking the helm as the fifth president of George Mason University in 1996, Dr. Alan Merten contemplated the many successes of his predecessor, Dr. George Johnson. Prior to Dr. Johnson, Mason had already seen three presidents in just six years of existence as an institution independent from the University of Virginia. Over his subsequent 18-year tenure, Dr. Johnson cultivated an environment of what Alan describes as "academic and institutional entrepreneurship", bringing the university to the brink of the 21st century as a leading institution in northern Virginia, known for feeding top candidates into the science, business and technology sectors in that region and beyond.

Alan's challenge was now to take Mason to the next level.

"Dr. Johnson's approach had created a situation where any flower could bloom," Alan remembers today. "He created the entrepreneurial George Mason University, and we had to keep that spirit, but we also had to create a certain order out if it." Alan asked himself not just, "How do we survive?" but, "How do we thrive?"

In 1996, Mason had approximately 21 thousand students. As of 2011 that number has grown to over 32 thousand, and the number of applicants continues to rise steadily each year. During Alan's tenure the university has built over twenty buildings across three campuses, and $5 million in sponsored research has grown to $120 million. "It's a different place," Alan allows today.

Born and raised in Milwaukee, Wisconsin, Alan earned his undergraduate degree in mathematics at the University of Wisconsin, where he was Air Force ROTC. After graduating, his first assignment in the Air Force was to obtain a master's degree in computer science from Stanford. Armed with this degree and still in his early twenties, he was first assigned to the Pentagon in the Air Force Data Services Center, then as a military aid to President Johnson. Later he would take on more responsibility, working in the White House as a social aid. Over three years these fascinating and demanding positions led him to become friends with Brian Lamb, founder and Chief Executive of CSPAN; Edward Mathias, Managing Director of the Carlyle Group; and others.

"Not much more can be said about my time at the Pentagon and the White house other than that it was a great experience, unlike any other I have had," he says. "But while working there I found myself getting more and more interested in various aspects of computer science and statistics." Following his four years in the Air Force, Alan returned to school, starting a PhD program in computer science at the University of Wisconsin.

While academic life as a career path was not something he had planned on, it became possible as he finished his PhD studies. Considering career options such as computer vendors, research groups and defense contractors, he ultimately chose academia and took an offer from the University of Michigan to teach there in Engineering and Management. It was not long after that he made the decision to take on more academic administration responsibilities, becoming an Associate Dean for Executive Programs at Michigan. After being at Michigan for sixteen years, he became dean of the business school at the University of Florida for three, then accepted a similar position at Cornell for seven.

With mounting experience in higher education administration, Alan came to a point where he found he had to decide whether to go back to the faculty, or to take the natural next step in his career as an administrator to become a university president. The decision would soon become much easier, as opportunity knocked in the form of a search firm looking to fill the presidency of George Mason University.

"It was exciting," he says. "I got involved in the Mason search, and as I went through the process it became clear to me that it was something I wanted to pursue... And that became possible."

Alan quickly realized that he was well-suited to the position. The search firm initially showed interest in him due to his background in computer science and his experience as a business school professor and dean. Together, these features made him a perfect fit for the northern Virginia environment and particularly Mason, with its reputation for producing highly qualified individuals in science and business who often found great success in Washington and beyond. Further, Alan had government and military-related experience even beyond his time in the Air Force from consulting for the military and other government bodies during his time as a professor.

As the process progressed through the end of 1995 and into 1996, and the number of finalists narrowed to ten and then four, Alan became confident that his academic background was consistent with the needs of the next level of George Mason University. "I had already begun to feel the synergy between what I wanted to do and what George Mason and the greater Washington area had to offer," he says. In June of 1996, George W. Johnson retired after eighteen years as University President, and Alan was inaugurated the following month.

Now, for President Merten, there is no such thing as a normal day. Indeed, every day, every hour looks different from the one preceding it. He describes his job by saying, "I am responsible for a $900 million organization every year. With an approximately $700 million operating budget, and a slightly less than $200 million capital budget, things start to get a little complex. In fact, we're spending $4 million a week on capital projects."

While Alan and his team say Mason is not a business and therefore isn't operated as such, they do run it in a "business-like fashion" to ensure stability, efficiency, and strength. In addition to the day-to-day responsibilities presented by thirty-three thousand students, six thousand employees, over one hundred buildings, and one hundred and forty thousand alumni, Alan must still envision strategies to address the greater challenges his university faces: how to manage a constantly increasing number of applicants, how to grow the university with uncertain support from the state assembly and governor, and how to enhance the university's capacity for high-quality research.

Despite these innumerable responsibilities, Alan is committed to being remarkably present in the lives of students, faculty, administrators, and university staff. In addition to understanding all aspects of a modern university, even those various aspects that may differ from the academic programs he has experienced himself, Alan stresses that a university president must also have an appreciation for the interests and demands of the students and for the communities that the university is a part of. "And that appreciation must be genuine," he adds. Those individuals who become academic administrators without that appreciation, who may try to fake it—those people will have failures."

The students at George Mason love that Alan is so visible. He models this leadership quality after a central theme of a particularly influential book in his life entitled, *In Search of Excellence*, by Tom Peters and Robert H. Waterman, Jr. To Alan, it is of the utmost importance to be visible among the students, to talk to the students, to listen to the students, and to be a part of their lives, with them an integral part of his in return. To this end, he participates in the two-day-long freshman move-in every year, introducing himself to parents and students alike, and he relishes their reactions. He attends as many basketball games as he can, both home and away, and as he sits at half court with his wife, a stadium of raucous students will regularly chant his name.

Though many academic professionals have to learn the importance of such integration over time, it has remained a cornerstone of Alan's philosophy since the beginning. "Through my academic career I always felt a need and an interest in getting to know the students outside the classroom," he says. "When I was dean at Florida, my wife and I would invite students to our home. When I was dean at Cornell, it was the same. We've always believed that students' experiences should extend far beyond a series of classes."

In his duties managing faculty and staff, Alan can be found implementing the same philosophy of "management by walking around," although he tends to take a more hands-off approach with those who work for him. He believes in giving people responsibilities and getting out of the way. "I try very, very hard not to micromanage," he notes. "I may have to bite my lip or other parts of my body, and I'd love to tell them how to do it, but I've learned over the years not to, and to trust people."

Looking at the university community as a whole, Alan says it is important to him to have respect for and a belief in people's abilities at all levels within the organization. "In a complex organization," he says, "the people at the top may be important, but the people far down the hierarchy are equally important." Whether it's the campus police, the maintenance staff, or a physical plant person, he makes it a point to walk up and thank them for their hard work. In his experience, this is not merely beneficial to his ability to manage, but it is integral to the functioning of the university as a whole. "To not do this is to miss an opportunity," he stresses.

In considering his tenure and the evolution of George Mason University as a whole, Alan sees a distinct progression. "My case is an example of one leader doing one set of things, and the next leader having to do the next set of things," Alan says. Recalling a recent interaction with the former president, Dr. George Johns, at the Mason Inn, a new hotel and conference center and one of the twenty or so new buildings constructed during Alan's tenure, Alan remembers a particularly telling exchange. "I walked up to Dr. Johnson and I said, 'George, what do you think of *this*?' We both took a moment to look around us, and he then looked at me and said, 'I could never have done what you've done.' I looked back at him and said, 'George, I could never have done what *you* did.'"

Though Alan's journey with Mason is far from over, it is already undeniably apparent that he will be remembered for his unique capacity to build institutions, not just in terms of the number of buildings he has constructed or the amount of fund-raising he has directed, but more so in the very legacy of the entity itself. Having invested so much of his focus, energy, and self into the institution, his individual impact is read in the amplification of Mason's impact as a whole. "Institutions consist of buildings," says Alan, "but institutions may also be understood in terms of the organizations we've created, the intellectual property we've developed, and the students who have succeeded. That is institution building, broadly stated."

Christos Papaloizou

Trusting the Flow

When Christos Papaloizou first started work as an evening busboy at a small Greek restaurant known as Taverna Cretekou, he was newly married and had just immigrated to America with his wife. Enrolled in full-time day courses to study heating, ventilation and air conditioning, he couldn't have guessed at the time that his part-time job would snowball into an engrossing, lucrative, and fulfilling career, but as he looks back now, he identifies this unpredictability as the beauty of it all. "I never thought I was going to be the owner of such a successful Greek restaurant," Christos muses today. "That's why you have to go with the flow, as they say. You never know what surprises life will bring you."

Having received a degree in accounting after studying for three years in London, it is evident that the restaurant business was never part of the young man's plan. In fact, Christos sought employment at Taverna

Cretekou because it promised fast money while he studied HVAC, and with a baby on the way, he couldn't afford to wait around. Though his venture was initiated for financial purposes, however, Christos knew from the outset that the contours of his soul were well matched for the industry. "I helped my mother-in-law with several of her restaurants before really committing to the industry, which gave me the opportunity to see that I loved meeting and getting to know all kinds of different people," he reflects. "The restaurant industry is perfect for that."

Christos's lovely wife, Denise, had been living in the U.S. prior to their fortuitous meeting on the beaches of his native Cyprus, where she visited each summer. The pair courted while Christos studied for his accounting degree, then married in Athens before coming to America on February 8, 1976. Taverna Cretekou had been established in 1974, and Christos worked there until 1978, when he departed for two years to assist his mother-in-law with several restaurants that she owned. At that point, he returned to Taverna Cretekou and was later promoted into a management role.

Christos managed the restaurant for about ten or fifteen years until the owner decided to sell the place, approaching Christos first to gauge his interest in buying it. "I couldn't have refused—the restaurant was like a baby to me," he recalls. "I grew up with this restaurant, and everybody here knew me. They thought I owned it long before I actually did," he laughs now.

Despite the very natural and innate nuance of his leadership, Christos had had no prior aspirations to own the enterprise, having always been happy and fulfilled in his position as manager. He'll never forget that day in 2005—among the biggest turning points of his life—when he assumed control not only of the restaurant, but of his own future as well.

"That's when I realized that the American Dream is still alive, at least for me," he explains. "I do feel that, in this country, whatever you believe can be done. After coming to America, I had always kept in my mind the question of how I could become a little bit more successful. We made investments and saved up gradually, which is what allowed us to buy the restaurant when the opportunity presented itself."

One pivotal change Christos instituted upon assuming ownership of the operation was to welcome Denise on as a vital member of his staff. Challenging the commonly held belief that husband and wife teams in the workplace spell certain doom, the two have proven to be a perfect pair in the professional sphere just as they have in a home environment. "Even if an owner and manager know each other well, one still cannot predict how the other will react when, as in the restaurant business, there are 20 different ways to do the same thing," Christos explains. "But you know your wife. If you have a problem, you solve it together, and I couldn't imagine anything better than that."

Through the Papalouizous' efforts, the business doubled with Denise at the front working as hostess and manager while Christos oversaw the books, purchasing, and other odds and ends. "I was surprised that we could so quickly improve upon a restaurant that had been run so well for so many years," he remarks. "These days, we're doing better than ever. As I said, it's like a baby. We feed and nurture it, and it grows gradually each year."

This success can be attributed in large part, as well, to the atmosphere of genuine friendship and family that permeates the Taverna Cretekou experience. It's no secret that the Papalouizous love their customers, and they strive to infuse each visitor's experience with personality and meaning, with Denise floating around the dining room throughout the evening to greet guests.

"We give our customers a smile when they come in, and we make sure that they leave with a smile as well," says Christos. "You have to make your customers happy, even with the small details. This is why I love picky customers. It's an opportunity to make someone happy. And if I can make them happy, my heart is happy. If someone comes in with a bad mood and leaves happy, then that's really something."

Perhaps the reason the restaurant has succeeded so considerably in treating its guests as family is because it is essentially a family-run atmosphere, with two of the Papaloizous' three children employed. Their daughter, Maria, manages the books, while their son, Nikos, will cook, manage the front, and run the Taverna if Christos and Denise are out of town. "He grew up helping me in the restaurant since he was 16 years old," Christos explains. "That's what you call a family restaurant!"

Still, he's very insistent that his children follow their own path, only welcoming them into the Taverna lifestyle if it's what they truly want for themselves. "No pressure," he says with a smile. "We're very lucky. We've found something we enjoy, we work, we make money, and life is beautiful."

Luck, enjoyment, and the other whimsical currents that have guided Christos's life are grounded by a strong work ethic, and this balance of work and whimsy has characterized his professional attitude since his very first job. Employed by his uncle, an electrician with his own business on the coast of Cyrpus, Christos and his cousins would work several hours in the morning and then spend the afternoon playing soccer on the beach. "I didn't care about the money because I had my cousins to play with, and that's all you really care about when you're a kid," he recalls fondly.

Christos was also very close with his parents. His mother was a high school principal and his father co-owned a construction business, modeling for their son the value of hard work and the joy of ownership. "My parents always believed in me," he recalls now. "I was very close with them. They didn't know what I would do, but they always knew that I had a good heart and that, down the road, I would be successful in something."

In fact, Christos's family contributed to the inception of his success just as much as they believed in it prior to his acquisition of the restaurant. This contribution was accomplished through the many life lessons he assimilated through observing them, many of which he continues to employ as a leader today. "My father and mother were very patient people, as is my wife," Christos points out as an example. "Having patience—that's what I'm trying to do now, like my father. It's especially important in the restaurant business to know how to maintain that element of peace and calm for both employees and customers." Christos also reflects on how his family's example of dealing with problems in an analytical and overarching fashion had a tremendous influence over him as well. "They always slow down and look at a problem from all angles, which has been a great thing for me," he explains.

Christos's example demonstrates that going with the flow can, as a strategy, mean so much more than simply rolling with the punches. When combined with an excellent work ethic, it means going through life with a unique and compelling blend of tranquility and conviction, openness and drive. "My grandfather always told me that, even if we learn something that isn't readily applicable today, we should put it aside and keep moving," Christos explains. "One day, it will come back and help you. For example, if I knew nothing about accounting and bookkeeping today, I'd definitely be in trouble."

By going with the flow and maintaining a committed yet laid back management style, Christos has experienced exceedingly low turnover since he took over Taverna in 2005. "I'm not a difficult person. Regardless of what life brings my way, I can adjust," he says, of his general demeanor. When applied to the workplace, this methodology makes for a low-stress yet high-efficiency atmosphere that exudes mutual respect and family-like cooperation. "My waiters, my chefs, every single person plays a little part in our success," Christos observes. "Not just me or my wife, but every single person. Everybody makes mistakes, but they are fixable, and it's beautiful for everybody. That's my philosophy."

Christos's philosophy also extends further, fomenting young entrepreneurs today with an approach to life that promises not only success, but also the deep-seated sense of joy that permeates his character. By not only going with the flow but also pursuing those things in life that allow one's true nature to flow freely through their work, one's full potential can be reached in a healthy and blissful way. "Choose your path not because of money or ego, but because of feeling and heart. Do what you love to do, and do it step by step, laying a firm foundation for your future," he urges.

By not only going with the flow, but trusting and enhancing it through heartfelt commitment and strong work ethic, one can achieve things that extend far beyond the trappings of a dream. "Even today, going on six years of ownership, my wife and I will sit down in the evenings after we've closed the restaurant," Christos imparts. "I still say to her, 'I never thought something like this would belong to us.'"

Danny Platt

The "Fix It" Frame of Mind

In today's increasingly specialized society, true "fix it" personalities are becoming somewhat of a rarity. When something breaks, we are apt to pick up the phone rather than troubleshoot ourselves. Danny Platt, however, was raised differently. "Innately, I'm a fix-it guy," he remarks, "and my life experiences have served to develop and accentuate that skill. I was raised with the kind of mindset in which, if you need something done, you do it yourself."

If Danny wanted something as a child, he was told to cut grass or shovel sidewalks to raise the cash to make it happen. Then, working in a family-owned deli in high school, he grew accustomed to fixing what was broken or solving what was wrong. Such an upbringing cultivates not only an outstanding self sufficiency, but an enduring sense of agency. Now the President and COO of LifeStar Response, his example demonstrates how the fix-it mentality holds as a lifelong key to success.

LifeStar is a $110 million private ambulance company that was founded as a family-owned bus company in the 1970s. The company underwent several acquisitions in the 1980s and 1990s, which included an ambulance company in Long Island. When the founder, Richard Gabriele, brought in several private equity groups in 1997 and closed the deal in 1998, they then commenced acquisitions outside of New York and New Jersey. The private equity took over the business in 2000 and has run it ever since, though Gabriele remains Chairman of the Board today. LifeStar now boasts 1,500 employees and 400 vehicles operating in seven states, providing nonemergency ambulance services in New York, New Jersey, Baltimore, and D.C., as well as nonemergency and emergency services in Alabama, Georgia, and Pennsylvania.

Danny grew up in the suburbs of Baltimore and attended Towson State University, where he met his long-time friend, Brad May. Brad's family owned a private ambulance business, and he convinced Danny to get his Emergency Medical Technician certification so the two could work there during the summers and on weekends while in college in 1984. "The class drew me in," Danny remembers. Impassioned by the experience of being in the ambulance and responding in a crisis, he began volunteering as a fire fighter and then received his certification as a paramedic, then working as a paramedic for the Baltimore City and Baltimore County Fire Department for ten years.

Though his commitment to emergency response remained unwavering, Danny couldn't deny the call of the fix-it aspect of his personality when the May family asked him to run the operations of their ambulance company. Accepting the position of Operations Manager for May Medical Transport in Baltimore marked his first foray into private business management, and with the company struggling at the time, Danny certainly had his work cut out for him. "You're much better off learning a business when it's in trouble than you are trying to learn it when things are good," he remarks now. "You learn a lot more that way."

It is often said that one cannot achieve tremendously if one does not risk tremendously, and Danny's story is the quintessence of the adage. Having always imagined that he'd spend 30 years with the Fire Department, making a nice living that afforded a comfortable retirement and a secure future, he'll never forget the day Brad approached him with the challenge to throw caution to the wind and take a risk by going into the private sector. "It was unheard of in my circle of acquaintances," Danny recalls. "Working for the Fire Department was a solid and rewarding experience, but I wasn't creating anything. I wanted to prove to myself that I could go out and create."

He thrived off the challenge until the Mays decided to sell the business to a national company several years later, cueing to Danny that it was time to move on. "My personality of operating in an entrepreneurial and aggressive fashion didn't mesh well with the process-oriented corporate culture of the new ownership," he recalls. "Though it was disappointing to me at the time that I couldn't adapt my personality to the role, I see in the long run that that it just wasn't me." He departed to work for Yellow Taxi in Baltimore for several years, at which time his friend Brad reached out to him again and urged him to come onboard with LifeStar.

When Danny started in June of 2000 as Director of Operations for LifeStar's Baltimore Washington market, the company in its entirety was only drawing $25 million in revenues. Of that, the Maryland market comprised $4 or $5 million and was bleeding $75 or $80 thousand per month. Danny was then told that he had until December to turn the region's tides, so he immediately shifted his concentration to the basics. "We went back to block and tackling," he reflects. "We knew that if we could repair our relationship with the employees and our relationship with the customers, then the financials would improve accordingly." True to form, the Baltimore Washington market was breaking even by December, and the upward trajectory continued steadily throughout the following years, with the market now drawing almost $30 million in annual revenue with 16 percent earnings.

Though Danny wasn't aware of how dire the situation was upon accepting his position at LifeStar, it is unlikely that a more acute awareness would have deterred him. In fact, it probably would have done just the opposite. "Being a fix-it and operations-oriented guy, I was attracted to the challenge," he explains. "At that point, I wasn't looking ahead at the prospect of becoming President. Rather, my main focus was on turning LifeStar into an operation we could all be proud of."

After the Baltimore Washington market showed such marked improvement, the CEO and the Board decided they would have Danny travel part-time to other operations to offer recommendations for change. After doing this for a year, however, he found that one had to be present full-time in order to ensure the implementation of these recommendations. Identifying the right people to run the businesses and oversee the implementation process then became a pivotal focus, and as these individuals were assimilated into the enterprise, LifeStar achieved a newfound stability that allowed its leadership to take a breath and consider what came next. From his experiences thus far, Danny had accrued a nuanced understanding not only of the company as a whole, but also of the unique stories that accompanied each of LifeStar's markets. "You can't take a cookie cutter approach to each location," he reports. "What works in Maryland doesn't work in Alabama. Each market has its own little story and you try to improve upon it, making it the best you can."

When Danny was then transitioned into the role of President in 2004, the progression felt organic and natural. "I transitioned from the kind of problem solving that involves trucks, supplies, and patients, to the kind of problem solving that involves numbers," Danny points out. "I'm still Mr. Fix-It, but now I fix things with numbers and a reasoning that is somewhat more abstract."

Regardless of whether he's developing solutions through hands-on, real-world solutions or through numerical analytics, Danny's leadership style has always been one of swift responsiveness and results-oriented action. "At big corporations, there's a lot of discussion that goes on," he reflects. "There's oftentimes a lot of red tape to get through. That's just not our company culture. Through our familiarity with and expertise of the industry, we can respond quickly, intuitively, and effectively, without much discussion."

To ensure that the LifeStar team is aligned and attuned to the company's goals, they conduct what Danny jovially refers to as "hallway meetings"—quick, focused exchanges when such discussion is necessary, rather than according to a weekly schedule. Jon Colin, the company's CEO, parallels Danny in this management philosophy. "We operate on the same personality wavelength," Danny comments. "We get things done quickly and don't waste a lot of time hashing over them. We're about action."

While this philosophy may exude an air of spontaneity, Danny actually attributes much of his success to the routine structure and discipline upon which his days are built. "Having a routine sets up my day to allow me to solve problems before they happen," he explains. "It's a focus on predictable chaos—being able to analyze the trends of any given situation through knowing what your indicators are." While seemingly at odds with the concept of hallway meetings, the two ideologies actually fit hand in hand. Having a routine helps to eliminate predictable chaos and ensure that LifeStar's leadership has a firm grasp on the variables of any given situation, and this in turn enables the team's quick, action-oriented response to any unpredictable chaos that might arise.

Beyond instituting the kind of behavioral structure that Danny illustrates here, he advises young entrepreneurs entering the workforce today to truly listen as they go about their daily lives. "To be successful at work, everyone always says one needs to work hard, but working hard at the *right* things is equally as important," he emphasizes. "Identify the key performance indicators that are important to a business and work toward helping those indicators improve."

Employing a fix-it mentality, then, is as much about fixing problems *before* they arise as it is about fixing them after they've developed.

Likewise, it's about taking a dire situation and turning it around one small problem at a time through intensive, interactive problem solving strategies. "I'm not afraid to get in the mess and work things out," says Danny. "This is how one's greatest challenge can be transformed into one's greatest success."

Richard Sawchak

To Whom Much is Given . . .

To all outward appearances, Richard Sawchak is the quintessential "company man", serving as the Chief Financial Officer of Paradigm Solutions, with a well-earned reputation of hard work and proven success. But when asked the most important thing that matters in his life, at the top of the list is family.

Sawchak's grandparents immigrated to the United States from Ukraine and settled in Northern Pennsylvania. Growing up in Scranton, Sawchak speaks of his father, "My dad's story is interesting. He never went to college, graduating high school at 16, and went straight into banking (in the equivalent of a teller) for his first position, and ended up retiring as the CEO of a small regional bank."

That same dedication and perseverance is evident in Sawchak's life. When remembering his plan for his future as a young man, Sawchak describes himself as being very goal-oriented. "I can remember when my wife and I first started dating, so I was 16, that the early parts of my plan for the future had started to be mapped. It was very much formalized before I graduated college, with literally, a goal for where I would be at 1 year, 3, 5, 10 and 15 years in my career."

Sawchak grew up knowing that his future career would more than likely be in the area of finance or banking, modeled after his father whose more than forty year career in banking influenced his son's industry of choice.

His father's influence also reached further than just career choice. Sawchak recalls his father's daily advice and guidance on life, "My dad said, 'You won't make the mistakes I made or the less optimal decisions that I made in these scenarios and these are the ones that turned out well for me, look at those and pattern after those'. So it was that mix of positive/negative analysis, this root cause analysis of his career and his life that my dad passed down to me."

Sawchak obtained his Bachelor of Science in Finance at Boston College in Chestnut Hill, Massachusetts and a Master of Science in Accounting at Babson College in Wellesley, Massachusetts. His high school sweetheart attended Boston College with him and just following graduation they became husband and wife. "We've been dating and married for twenty-one years and married for fifteen years," Sawchak says with a smile, "marrying her was the best decision of my life. I married up, pretty heavily."

After graduation, Sawchak was hired to perform Mergers and Acquisitions (M&A) analysis at Lucent Technologies, a telecommunications corporation. While at Lucent, Sawchak was always working on the critical issues and was often given the opportunity to grow but he didn't feel as if the large company bureaucracy and politics allowed him the ability to make a measurable impact on the company.

After working at Lucent for four years, Sawchak decided to go the complete opposite route and took a position at a small start-up company, Multilink Technology Corporation.

"I went from being one of one hundred sixty thousand employees to less than one hundred fifty employees and from $30 billion in revenue to a little less than $30 million in revenue."

Sawchak describes his experience at Multilink as exciting. "There was no policy in place, no discipline, no structure, no process. I was brought in to build that infrastructure," Sawchak continues, "I found that every day I could actually touch and physically move forward a list of things within the company. I could see the exact thumbprint that I was putting on the company and how I was helping it to make strides forward."

In the small company environment, Sawchak thrived. "If you had asked me at the time if I would always stay at small companies for the rest of my career, my answer would have been, 'Yes, this is exciting. I want to be helping small companies find their path to growth and success'."

In 2003, Multilink was sold and Sawchak and his wife moved to Maryland so that he could fill the Director of Finance position at GXS, Inc., a global finance organization focused on improving business performance. Though GXS was a larger company than Multilink, Sawchak felt that he could still feel that everyday impact. "GXS had some of the elements of both a small start-up like Multilink and a larger corporation like Lucent," explains Sawchak.

In 2005, Sawchak was approached by a professional recruiter to interview for the Chief Financial Officer position at Paradigm Solutions, a newly-public corporation providing IT services to civilian agencies of the federal government.

When interviewing for the position at Paradigm, Sawchak recalls many viable candidates for the role. "M&A, corporate finance, and fundraising were always on my plate so by the time that I got to Paradigm, that was something that I had done for a number of companies over a number of years." But Paradigm was, at its core, a government contractor and Sawchak had no experience in that arena.

When asked by the Paradigm executives why he should be considered when he wasn't a "federal guy", Sawchak recalls his response, "I was in telecommunications and we were somewhat regulated there, and I've been in public companies my whole life and we were regulated by the SEC there, you're just talking about a different set of regulations. I'll sit down and I'll learn the regulations, but from a business perspective, you have other people in your company who know the federal business and the rules there and what you need. What you don't have is a person with the skill set of an M&A or a public company perspective, who can help you to drive and build a strategy to figure out where the company is supposed to go next, and I can bring those attributes from day one."

That perspective and skill set convinced Paradigm that Sawchak was the right person for the job and he has been with the company ever since. Though Paradigm is a larger company than Multilink, Sawchak still finds that small-company excitement each day. "At Paradigm, it is more like that everyday fight at Multilink that I enjoyed."

When asked about his unwavering work ethic and his success, Sawchak credits three driving forces behind his dedication: early goal-setting and follow-through, his father's devotion to family, and Sawchak's overwhelming desire to make his father proud.

Sawchak explains that once he had set his goals, then failure became unacceptable to him. He says, "For me it was an internal drive of saying, 'I wrote down this list, I have goals and things I want to achieve, and my wife and I have made commitments to ourselves and we know where we want to be in our lives and what we want to be able to do from a personal perspective, a family perspective, a charitable perspective.' To not put in the hours and the effort to make sure that our goals are met—I felt that it's better to be ahead of schedule than behind schedule."

When speaking of his father's focus on family, Sawchak recalls, "I watched my dad stay at the same place, stay in a smaller town, stay at a smaller bank, and looked at him with his level of intelligence and his level of ability and always thought as I grew up that he cut himself short and that he could have done so much more. I remember looking at the executives, early on in my career, that I was rubbing shoulders with and thinking, 'my dad is better than that', but yet he had put his family first and chose to not worry as much about his career and I thought that I didn't want to do that."

His father's approval was another of Sawchak's strong motivations, "I watched my dad smile every time I accomplished and every time I clicked through one of my markers, I saw happiness and approval in his eyes. It gave me sort of an adrenaline rush, in allowing him to enjoy it when I succeeded. It was important to me that he know that his choice to put the family first made this all possible for me."

Though Sawchak has a stalwart work ethic and knows how to burn the midnight oil, he too puts an emphasis on family. "As enjoyable as career is and I like my car and I like my house, those things are nice, but in the long run they don't really matter." Family comes first.

Sawchak and his wife put family first in their own way, deciding early on in their courtship that they would focus on career during the first ten years of their marriage and save children until later. They decided that they would benefit from their own childhood experiences with growing up and parenthood, to provide the best possible experience for their child. So, after a successful career in marketing, once they were ready for children, Sawchak and his wife decided that she would stay home to raise their family.

Not only is Sawchak focused on family and career, but he also has a sincere drive to give back. He sits on the Board of Trustees for Valley Forge Christian College (VFCC) in Pennsylvania, volunteers with the Youth Group at his church, and donates to his alma mater, Boston College.

When describing his charitable work at VFCC, Sawchak relates, "I didn't go to VFCC and I even used to make fun of it because it is a small college and it is underwhelming. But I looked at my life one day, and I looked at the many people who had poured into my life and helped me over time and what I found was that many of those friends and relationships were with graduates of VFCC. And so what I realized was that I wouldn't be where I am today without that college. It was not my alma mater, but it was the alma mater that created people who helped me. I felt the need to become involved with the college so that the next 'me', who wouldn't be here today without that college, would get to be here."

"I'm thankful for what God has blessed me with," Sawchak explains, "I am very fortunate—I have a great family, I've had a great career, I have a beautiful home, a great car and I'm proud of my dad and I'm proud of my wife and daughter."

Sawchak's leads his life in accordance with the bible verse, "To whom much is given, much is required." He says, "I have been blessed with more than anybody I know and so to not give back, would be unconscionable."

When looking to the future, Sawchak envisions his time after retirement as being when he can focus on more charitable work and non-profits. "I want to be that guy who made the transition from the pure corporate world to taking these skill sets and that network and knowledge-base and applying it to those groups who need the help but don't often get it because they can't afford it. If I could get to that point, I would be very happy."

Richard Sawchak has had a truly blessed career, being led to ever increasing roles at companies and with co-workers that spurred him to do more and to accomplish more. Led by his father's engrained work ethic and detailed planning for the future, Sawchak has carved out a piece of the American pie that so many dream of. His father's ultimate goal realized, Sawchak stands poised to finish out his career, retiring by the age of 55, and being able to focus on mentoring, giving back, and his continued duty to family first.

When asked his message to new graduates, Sawchak advises, "Focus now, hunker down, grab every experience and every mentor you can. Get to know people, build your network, and create the foundation for you, your family, and your friends for down the road. There is a saying, 'no good foundation, no good house', because if you build the foundation strong, the house stands well on it."

Sawchak has planned, implemented, and built his foundation strong. He has put family first, honored his father and mother, his wife and daughter, and has built a reputation and a work ethic that is unrivaled. He gives back, mentors the next generation, and never forgets the lessons that he has learned along the way. Sawchak has built his 'good foundation' and we are seeing just how well his house stands.

Randy Schools

Making a Living through Making a Change

With a heart that was not only heavy, but literally ailing, Randy Schools sighed in the hospital bed where he had spent the past two weeks. Surburban Hopsital is amongst the best healthcare facilities in the world, yet not even their top-notch physicians could ascertain the proper diagnosis. Having lost his mother at an early age, Randy now looked over at his father sitting opposite him in the sterile hospital room, his spirit at a loss.

"God," he said, "if I make it out of this, I'm going to take my life in a different direction."

It wasn't that there was anything inherently wrong with working 70-hour weeks as an operations manager at Garfinckel's, a chain in the DC metro area. It was just that Randy had always felt in his gut that his life's work lay somewhere else, and with the whispers of mortality haunting his mind, he prayed he would have a little more time to pursue a path that meant more to him. If there were a future in store for Randy's professional accomplishments, it would no longer be enough to make a living. From that moment onward, Randy vowed he would make a change.

Miraculously, the symptoms of Randy's mysterious heart condition began to dissipate a week later. His doctor came in the following Saturday to take him on a jog to assess his strength, and when Randy was at last pronounced healthy enough to be discharged, it seemed as though he had been given the chance he had asked for. Not only had he received the gift of time, but also the gift of fortuitous direction: before leaving Surburban Hospital, he learned that The National Institutes of Health (NIH), which was right across the street, was looking for someone to fill the general manager vacancy for its Recreation and Welfare Association. Now that Randy serves not only as the President of that enterprise, but also of NIH Charities, his is a story of finding one's true path in life and the perseverance it takes to follow it.

NIH has roughly 25,000 employees operating out of its DC, Baltimore, and Montana locations, and its Recreation and Welfare Association serves to boost the morale and quality of life for those individuals by operating gift shops, wellness and fitness programs, and special interest groups like sailing, volleyball, and basketball leagues. Randy leads a team of 35 employees, and the association generally does between $1.5 and $2 million in revenues annually.

After commencing his career with NIH in 1977, a parent of a patient lost his daughter to cancer and soon approached Randy with the vision of launching a summer camp for children afflicted with the illness. Randy had gotten his Certified Association Executive credential, which gave him some expertise in founding nonprofits, so they began with a small group of 33 kids from NIH and local hospitals. The project, called Camp Fantastic, now hosts around 400 children at any given time and operates about 30 programs.

"Working with Tom and Sheila Baker to launch Camp Fantastic was probably one of the best decisions of my life," Randy affirms now.

"Embarking on the journey to create that first nonprofit was the catalyst to grow other charities. It was like planting a seed." That seed eventually grew into Randy's next charitable endeavor, called Friends of The Clinical Center, which provides financial assistance to families in distress through short-term assistance such as car or house payments.

This program was then followed by the Children's Inn, a 55-room facility on the NIH campus providing housing for individuals participating in long-term NIH protocols. These initiatives were promoted through the charity's fundraising efforts, which have evolved to include galas and golf tournaments, but the real turning point for NIH Charities came when the CEO of Merck & Co. suddenly got involved by providing funding for the initiatives. Having been a young doctor at NIH himself and wanting to give back, he was instantly meeting fundraising goals that would have otherwise taken the Charities years to accumulate.

Randy's role in the creation and facilitation of NIH Charities reflects a commitment to giving back that was forged in his character long ago. "I can still remember Thanksgivings," he reflects. "My Uncle Calvin dined with the family infrequently, but instead spent the holiday working at a homeless shelter. That was something that really stuck with me as a kid."

Randy hails from a working class background, and each summer his father would drive him far beyond the streets of Baltimore to watch the Baltimore Colts sweat through their practice training camps at Westminster College. One of his best memories was watching Johnny Unitas and Raymond Berry practice, both of whom later went on to have Hall of Fame careers. "I remember how they would run sprints between trees, over and over," he muses. "I observed how the players who stayed after the ending of the regular practice were the ones who got really good. It was a powerful, immediate lesson in perseverance."

This lesson soon proved invaluable when he began his coursework at the University of Baltimore, working 40-hour weeks on top of the 16 credits he took per semester. He had been no stranger to hard work in the past, having worked as an usher for his Uncle Calvin, who at that time worked in the racehorse industry. Calvin had been a tremendous role model for young Randy, and a steely work ethic and focus seeped into him throughout his young employment. He was later hired to work in a men's clothing store called Websters, and by his senior year of college, he had become the store manager.

Randy graduated from college amidst the upheaval of the Vietnam era and had received his draft notice during his junior year, so he began counterintelligence work along with 48 other young men. Those 48 were assigned overseas, however, Randy miraculously found himself assigned to the White House, where his work in background investigations soon evolved into special operations. "They bought me a tuxedo, and I did undercover work," Randy reports. "It was great in that I got to meet celebrities and political leaders, but it was rough because you don't have complete control over your life. In the mornings I couldn't just say, 'Bye honey, see you tonight.' Instead, it was more like, 'Bye honey, see you tonight or in a week or who knows when.' It was very rough on a young marriage."

It was for these reasons that Randy decided to curb his counterintelligence work and instead commence the career with Garfinckel's that would cause him to reexamine his life when faced with his heart ailment several years later. The chain was a good career choice for Randy at the time, but NIH held a unique draw for him. "Even back then, it was a very international community," he reflects. "People from all over the world come to work and research at NIH, and I really thrive on meeting people from different cultures. This is also true of the patient community. It's an education in itself just to be there, and I'm always working with very bright people."

Randy learned the importance of curiosity and flexibility in the work environment at an early age, but it wasn't until he commenced his career with NIH that he truly grasped that the best leaders aren't afraid to relate to their workforce on a level playing field. "Anyone in a management position must still be willing to dig the trenches, unload a truck, and really be working alongside the people you're supervising," Randy points out. "Never assume you're better than anyone else, and along those same lines, never assume somebody else is better than you. Don't put people up on pedestals, but instead strive to find common ground so you can really work together and make things happen."

Leveraging this vision has taken Randy far, but it's actually a different kind of vision that he emphasizes as among the most important ideas when advising young entrepreneurs entering the business world today. "Try to look not at what the world is like right now, but at what you think it will be like in the next ten to twenty years," he urges. "Pursue the skills you forecast will be most relevant, and figure out how to communicate your vision to others so they can have a better life too." Beyond this, Randy emphasizes the importance of a renaissance knowledge base in a world that seems to be getting smaller by the day. "They say that our fathers' generation grew up in the context of villages, ours is growing up in the context of cities, and our children's will grow up in the context of the world," he explains. "Try to cultivate an independence and a cultural awareness that will keep you competitive, even in this broad domain."

While Randy's explicit lessons convey a work environment that is inherently competitive, his own example also stresses the overarching importance of our connections to and responsibility toward one another. "Despite these tough economic times, I think a better future is possible," he affirms optimistically. "The determining factor in whether or not we make it there will be our ability to adopt core values. Good citizens take care of all members of society, and good corporate citizens with the ability and wherewithal to help others absolutely have a responsibility to do so. We're facing a new, all encompassing kind of teamwork now."

Teamwork. Quality of life. Serving the underserved. Brightening the lives of the ill and the lives of those who care for them. When Randy

Schools was given another chance at life, he decided to start making his living by making a difference. If you were given another chance too, might you perhaps choose to do the same?

M.N. Scott Ulvi

Planning to Prosper

"Are you crazy?" That was the question Scott Ulvi's friend posed to him when he said he was serious about starting his own business.

"You've got two kids in high school, and college is right around the corner. Why would you take that kind of financial risk?" his friend pressed.

Scott hadn't looked at it that way until that moment. It wasn't that he hadn't considered all of his options; in fact, he had analyzed them quite thoroughly. It was just that failure wasn't among them.

Using the equity that remained in his house, he boldly invested in the startup costs, and when the housing market began to plummet just a few months later, he knew he wouldn't have had the means to get the company off the ground if he had waited. Now the President and CEO of Triumph Enterprises, Inc., a 75-employee contracting firm that closed at just over $11 million in sales for 2010, Scott's belief in his own convictions is, in itself, a triumph. "I don't see obstacles as problems, but as opportunities," he points out. "That's how I view life in most instances, and especially in business. Even if it's just a learning opportunity, it's an opportunity none the less."

At its inception, Triumph Enterprises aimed to provide professional management services to various government entities, with its main focus being the Department of Defense (DoD). Scott incorporated the idea in early 2005 and began hiring his first employees in February of 2006 when Triumph received its first contracts. One such hires was Joe Maurelli, who shared the same philosophy and the same objective—to create a phenomenal small business that leveraged what they had learned in their careers to improve both large and small companies. "Our concept was to create the next generation of federal management services company to provide program and project management services to the federal government," Scott explains. "We wanted our company to be good at everything that we decided to do and great in a few key areas."

He grew up the oldest of six children in a family of modest means. College was never discussed in the Ulvi household, and Scott knew it wasn't in the cards for him, so when he crossed paths with a Navy recruiter shortly after graduating high school, he promptly signed up for a six-year commitment. "I didn't even get out of boot camp before realizing that the Navy wasn't for me," Scott remarks now. "Still, I stuck with it for five years until I blew my knee out and was placed on medical hold."

After he underwent surgery for his injury, Scott was discharged from the Navy and married his wife Toni, whom he had met in Mayport. Though he had been trained on radar systems, he instead hoped to build a graphic design business, but as fate would have it, he was asked to interview for a position with a defense contracting company in Washington, DC. "My wife had lived in the Jacksonville, FL area all her life, so it was a big transition," he reports. Within a year of relocating to Germantown, MD, their first daughter Paige was born, and Scott soon realized that he couldn't afford to raise a family in the DC metro area making only ten bucks an hour.

His supervisors, nodding in agreement, gave him permission to work all the overtime he needed to earn enough cash, so Scott found himself sweating through 14-hour days just to pay the bills. "I certainly wasn't a hard worker growing up," he reflects honestly. "The work ethic I displayed wasn't inherent, but bred of circumstance. When we moved to DC, it was sink or swim, and I had my family depending on me."

Scott remained with that company for over two years, and because of his strong loyalty streak, he likely would have remained there indefinitely had his contract been extended. As it was, however, he could no longer work the overtime he needed to make ends meet, so he began looking for his next step. "Life presents us all with moments where we have to make difficult decisions, and that was certainly one of them for me," he reflects now. "Fortunately, the contracting business is all about relationships, and I had a customer from my prior position who believed in me and wanted to help me out."

That customer paved the way for Scott to acquire his next position, which he held for 11 years until that company was acquired by Anteon. After staying on for several years longer, he realized it was time to make his next career move, but wasn't sure exactly what that move should be. "Every time I've come to a turning point in my life, someone has been there to guide me to that next opportunity," he marvels now. "I've never been a hundred percent qualified for any of the jobs I've acquired, but that has always just inspired me to work harder because I never want to let down that person who gave me the opportunity."

It was in accordance with this idea that Scott accepted an offer of employment when he was invited to run the DoD's Mentor-Protégé Program, and he was soon serving in that capacity with as much skill as if he had done it all his life. "I loved everything about the program and how it was about people helping people," he affirms. "It was about companies helping other companies to take their current abilities and accelerate them." Scott himself mentored seven companies in the five years he served as Program Manager, and in that time he acquired a wealth of invaluable first hand experience across a broad spectrum of successes and failures.

"I had observed all sorts of regular people doing all sorts of irregular things and engendering all manner of results, and I decided to do something with that intelligence," he confirms. "I really thrived from being around entrepreneurs—people who were big thinkers and big risk-takers. Seeing so many others pursue their entrepreneurial goals gave me the confidence to try it myself." Scott left behind his role as a Mentor in the Mentor-Protégé Program in 2002 but has continued to support the DoD with this program ever since, and the myriad lessons he learned continue to enrich his professional journey. Ray Lopez, the CEO of Engineering Services Network, and one of his former Protégé companies, hired him on for several years; subsequently, Triumph was born.

Triumph is now 8(a) certified and is designated as a Service-Disabled Veteran-Owned Small Business, but perhaps the most remarkable and lucrative concept behind its operation is the fact that Scott has been leading his team in accordance with a Ten Year Plan. Such forward-thinking roadmaps are remarkably scarce in the business community, as many business owners lead such hectic lives that they are forced to live year-to-year and even month-to-month. "To determine this plan, I looked at my age, my family, and where we were in our lives," Scott explains. "I knew I had to persevere, even when people would say I couldn't do it. My wife was 100 percent supportive, and knowing my family was counting on me was a huge incentive to succeed."

While the first five years of his ten-year vision have been about surviving, the success that Triumph has already achieved suggests that the next five will be about thriving. In fact, Scott has his sights set on evolving the company into a $100 million enterprise by the end of 2015. "I rarely hit the targets I set for myself because they're so aggressive, but

I'm usually close," he explains. "Setting goals in this fashion ensures that I'm always pushing myself to the limits and beyond instead of adjusting the expectations I have for myself."

Though Scott has accumulated a vast portion of his knowledge stores through the professional experiences of his past, it comes as somewhat of a surprise that some of his most valuable business lessons were learned not in the office, but at home. Raising his two teenage daughters Paige and Brooke, for instance, has figured prominently into his leadership philosophy and has made him a better developer of others. "In my mind," he explains, "leadership is less about leading and more about listening and about helping people achieve what they want to achieve while keeping them focused on what it is that I, as the leader of the enterprise, am trying to achieve for the good of the company. In this sense, parenting has been the most important leadership training I've had."

In advising young entrepreneurs entering the workforce today, Scott echoes the same advice he's given the daughters that have taught him so much, which is to find the thing you love to do and do it. "If the thing you love to do doesn't produce tremendous wealth, so be it," Scott challenges. "True passion comes from within and is not externally motivated. Find out what it is that you wake up in the morning and are excited to do, and then seek out every instance where you can create an opportunity to engage in those things you're truly passionate about."

Beyond creating opportunities to pursue passion in one's life, Scott also highlights the importance of creating opportunities to pursue knowledge. This can be done through actively choosing to spend time with people who inspire progress and success through their examples and perspectives. "Spend a lot of time listening and paying attention to what's going on around you in people—what they're thinking, what motivates them, and what you can learn from them," he urges. "I can't think of anything more informing than those you choose to spend your time with. My best business decision, by far, has been to surround myself with the right people."

By employing these strategies in his own life, Scott and his team have created a company that has accomplished things in its fledgling five-year existence that many companies don't achieve in a decade. "We're proud of this evolution," says Scott. "It is my thinking that companies should take their first handful of years to gain solid proficiency at being a business and delivering service, and should then focus on improving, improving, improving. Because we're so process-focused, it's great for us to recognize that many of these processes have already reached that improvement stage, while the others are nearing it." Aiming for perfect and emerging somewhere in that vicinity, Scott's example is a testament to the practice of preparing, of planning, and ultimately, of prospering.

Thomas Verghese

A Well-Rounded Perfection

As a child growing up in New Delhi, the capital of India, Thomas Verghese understood that life was about extremes. These extremes lay not only in the minutely focused school day, which essentially lasted from five in the morning until ten at night through hundred-degree heat, but also in the filtering process that students underwent from an early age.

The first choice children were expected to make was that between sports and academics. "In America, you're encouraged to be well rounded, but in India, you have to be like an arrow, constantly aimed and shooting toward what you want—that singular goal," he recalls. "It was my passion early on to be the best, so that's what I was constantly striving for." Now a managing partner of SAXON Infotech, Inc., a growing software and research company based out of Columbia, Maryland,

Thomas still aims for perfection, but the way he defines this term has acquired new depth and nuance over the years.

Confronted with that initial decision, Thomas chose to commit his faculties toward academics, and by the time he reached tenth grade, he had situated himself well on the track to pursuing a future in the sciences. By the time he reached twelfth grade, the separation process had been complete. Those aiming for a highly competitive slot at one of the best schools, like Thomas, had been siphoned off into one class, separated from others who hadn't made the cut. "Those last two years of grade school in India are among the most competitive you can imagine," he reminisces. "If you want to embark on an upward trajectory, you have to really perform during that timeframe."

Steadfastly committed and fueled by his passion for excellence, Thomas earned himself admittance to the Indian School of Technology, Delhi to study engineering, having been one in about 200 thousand applicants competing for a spot at the esteemed institution. Upon graduating, he spent three years working for a $2 billion company. The experience was somewhat unusual for an engineering graduate in that it focused more on sales and business development, but nothing could have been more fortuitous for young Thomas. "It was exciting in the sense that you could see the flow of revenue, and that fascination stayed with me," he reports now.

Driven by that spark and his lifelong interest in continued learning, he again competed against the best of the best and won a spot at the Indian School of Management, Ahmedabad, currently ranked eleventh in the world in its field. "Getting an MBA is extremely useful for running a business, especially a small or mid-sized company, because you can see the enterprise end to end," he explains. "You come to see that working capital is your lifeline and to understand how revenue flows."

Having honed his skills with such intention, Thomas wondered when he would start his own business. Entrepreneurship ran deep in his family history, with successful traders and merchants peppering his lineage. Through his corporate experience with General Electric and MMTC thus far, he had come to understand that giving people freedom in the workplace maximizes their productive potential, as he himself preferred to do independent work in which he reported primarily to himself, and he looked forward to incorporating this approach into his own leadership style someday. "I've always had a passion to start something and to do something of my own," he reveals.

Swallowing his entrepreneurial dreams for the time being, though, Thomas came to the U.S. to earn his advanced degree in information systems from Carnegie Mellon. "In a broad sense, I understood that the world was in the process of being shaped by information systems," he explains, "but I'm the kind of guy who really likes to dig into the details at a fundamental level. This is where I feel most comfortable; it's a source of power for me."

Having earned a degree that would impart this comprehension of detail, Thomas accepted a position as Director of Research at CredAbility, a financial and debt management services firm in Atlanta, Georgia. In this capacity, his skills were challenged as he explored business intelligence, information structuring, and data trends, reviewing client profiles for patterns so that he could best understand the issues they were facing and thus recommend meaningful service improvements to the company.

It wasn't until three years later, when Thomas crossed paths with an old acquaintance, that his entrepreneurial spirit again began to stir. Shibu Jose had also come over to the states from New Delhi, and in 2005, he launched SAXON in accordance with his dream of starting a software company. Thomas, however, was more impassioned by the prospect of building something all their own. "Yes, I have a degree in engineering, but I'm much more interested in setting up a business and its structure," he reports, voice full of enthusiasm. "While Shibu is more well know for the technological aspects, I was most excited about building the company from scratch."

Pragmatic and somewhat risk-averse in his approach, Thomas kept his job with CedAbility while helping to mold SAXON on the side, only taking the full leap to SAXON in 2009 when its profits had stabilized. "I like to jump into what I'm doing, but once I do, I fall into it completely," Thomas explains. "I like to fully weigh the pros and cons, ensuring that I make a soundly rational decision before entering into anything."

When he first came fully on board, the enterprise lacked skeleton and structure, functioning as best it could without any systems in place. Leveraging the strategic thinking skills that set him apart, Thomas swiftly commenced securing a professional accounting group for SAXON, as well as an effective marketing strategy. "It's my job to do all the foundational steps in terms of making sure the appropriate systems are in place as the company matures," he explains. "With these systems, I'm ensuring that the company is growing revenue-wise, as well as diversifying and maintaining the interests of our client base."

SAXON originally started as an IT placement company securing highly qualified consultants for Fortune 500 companies, as the market for such services in 2005 was lacking. "If you were looking for someone with a very specific skill, it was hard to find those individuals, so we sought to fill that void," Thomas explains. Then, as the market shifted, they looked inwardly as well as outwardly to determine how they could differentiate themselves amidst shifting terrain and demands. Shibu's information architecture skills had gained considerable renown, so the firm picked up project management services to supplement its placement expertise.

With eyes still to the horizon, SAXON then underwent additional evolution by recognizing the wealth of untapped knowledge possessed by its staff. Shibu and Thomas thus decided to further differentiate themselves by adding research to their repertoire, exploring the horizons of software application creation and boundaries. "In this capacity, we're contributing to a product which might become a success down the road, so it's a long-term investment," says Thomas. It is without a doubt that the competitive spirit so deeply ingrained in Thomas throughout his childhood has come to the aid of SAXON today in this fashion, maintaining its poise on the cutting edge of the industry. "This is real life, and it's competitive," he continues. "In a free market economy, it's hard to compete on rate because other companies can always outsource. As such, we prefer to compete on quality."

Competing on quality in this manner, SAXON has chiseled out quite a name for itself, boasting 25 employees and revenues of just under $10 million. In addition to Fortune 500 companies and other commercial clients, they now serve the Federal government as well. Thomas also envisions an aggressive growth plan over the next several years, aiming to increase the workforce to 100 and the revenues accordingly. "That is our goal, but above all, this needs to be a place where people enjoy doing the work and have an appropriate work-life balance," he emphasizes.

This slight relaxing of his otherwise stick-straight standards does not so much represent a departure from perfection, but rather a revamping of its meaning. With one daughter already and his wife Litty and him expecting another, Thomas's management philosophy has come to embrace a more balanced ideal—one that acknowledges the human side of a workforce and the fact that employees, too, have families. Keenly tuned into the current recession and its implications for financial security, he recognizes that even after a lifetime of ultra-competitiveness, one really has power only over one's own efforts. "You can't really control what happens to the fruits of your labor," he points out. "All you can really control is whether or not you do your best."

"As long as we are financially stable and delivering the highest quality product to our clients, relaxing a little and broadening our horizons is a good thing," Thomas continues. "A company's people are its biggest assets, and time is their greatest resource. People should use it to pursue things that interest them." Thomas, himself, is tremendously well read in the arts, philosophy, and literature, and continues to delve deeper into such topics, using his own free time to launch an internet portal of collaboration and discussion entitled MyCulturalIndia.com. "Life doesn't always need to be about violence and power play," he affirms.

In advising young entrepreneurs entering the business world today, Thomas lists first and foremost the importance of setting goals. "This is a very difficult process, and you need to evaluate it carefully," he cautions. "Start thinking early about what you're passionate about and what differentiates you from others." Beyond this, he emphasizes the fact that we are all essentially competing globally now. "Don't get too focused on your immediate environment, because there's a whole world out there," he advises. "Be competitive, yet be balanced, and in achieving the goals you have in life, don't sacrifice the art of living."

Richard Vernon

A Family Man

When asked how he would most like to be remembered, Thurgood Marshall said, "As someone who did the best he could with what he had." Rick Vernon not only admires this legacy, but *lives* it, taking what comes most naturally to him and building a life of success and impact upon these strong foundations. A partner for more than 21 years with Lerch, Early, & Brewer, a preeminent regional law firm in Montgomery County, Maryland, he got to where he is today through his innate ability to bring the best out of people and spin it into meaningful relationships, whether the material of these relationships is friendship, business, or family.

In the 61 years since its inception, the law firm of Lerch, Early & Brewer has expanded to more than fifty attorneys dispersed across twelve discrete practice areas that include corporate, tax, litigation, Montgomery County real estate, health care, trusts and estates, domestic law, homeowner association practice matters, and employment and labor law. Rick joined the firm in December of 1990, immediately distinguishing himself through his launch of the employment and labor group, which he currently co-chairs. The group represents management exclusively in all matters involving employment and the workplace, supplementing this focus through servicing senior corporate executives with counsel on employment or severance agreements.

"The quality of attorney here is amazing," Rick marvels. "Coupled with a culture of respect at all levels, Lerch Early is a wonderful place for a lawyer to work. At its root, the culture stems from Harry Lerch, whose father was among the firm's original founders. Harry is the consummate gentleman, and he's maintained a gentle and refined composure without fail throughout the 21 years I've known him." This is not to say, however, that Harry Lerch's courteous demeanor was never tested. Indeed, the firm dropped from thirty-eight lawyers to only twenty in 1990, plagued by practices that went flat or relocated. The board of directors was replaced with a fresh cast of individuals committed to operating the firm as a true business, and as Rick puts it, "it has been a wonderful sleigh ride ever since." The firm emerged from those dark times and enjoyed particularly meteoric growth from 2006 through 2008, continuing to flourish in the years since then even despite the recession that followed. "We've been able to maintain a very good, effective, vibrant business, and this is thanks to the great quality of our lawyers across the board," Rick explains.

Rick's education began at Haverford College and was continued at Columbia Law School, where he had a strong academic record but not a perfect one. He established a sense of balance and prioritization early on which is still evident in his life today, and in adhering to this respect for balance, his heart told him to go with an agency rather than a law firm straight out of school. "I had this inkling that I should further my own education at a government agency in order to make myself a prime candidate for law firms later on," he remembers. Thus, he launched his law career with the National Labor Relations Board (NLRB) in D.C., which gave him the labor field expertise that today proves so valuable in his current role.

Rick's hunch proved accurate. After five years with the NLRB, during which the organization relocated him and his young family to Philadelphia, he was picked up by a premier management-side labor law firm in Philly. Two years later, he left that firm to accept a position with a smaller firm back in the D.C. area. Up to this time, his practice had been restricted primarily to matters that involved dealing with unions. Rick later worked for Epstein, Becker, & Green, which gave him the opportunity to delve into the other facet of management-side labor law that included discrimination and other workplace claims. "Dealing with people is at the essence of employment law, more so than nearly every other field of law," he remarks. "It's about conflict between people, and I took to this early on."

Feeling as though he was ready to run his own department, Rick transitioned over to a Baltimore-based firm and worked on creating an employment law practice in their D.C. regional office. However, he disagreed with the firm's passive marketing stance, which revolved around the idea that clients will come to you if you simply excel at what you do. "I was in the throes of learning at the time, trying to go out and generate my own client base," Rick recalls. "After five years, it was going well, but I decided that I wanted something more." It was around this time that he learned from a headhunter that Lerch, Early aimed to launch an employment practice.

Rick gave Lerch, Early, & Brewer more serious consideration when he realized that its client dealings were primarily with employers in the suburban area rather than in downtown Washington. Both Rick and the firm took a chance on one another, and both couldn't have been more right in doing so. "It really feels that this is the place where I truly belong, and I'll be here until I retire," Rick affirms confidently. The rest is, or will be, history.

Though his clients would not hesitate to speak of his strong grasp of the law and exceptional legal counsel, what has really set Rick apart in building and maintaining his law practice are his people skills. "I'm pretty good at rubber chicken dinners," he laughs, referring to his natural ability to befriend strangers and engender relationships at trade association and other large get-togethers. "I'm not afraid to reach out my hand and say hi. Good contacts are truly made through the one-on-one." Equipped with this knowledge, he has been known to pick up employer clients as he's out walking his dog, jogging, or running errands around the community. "My next aim is to meet a client on an elevator," he says with a wink.

Rick's infectious sense of humor and positive energy are invaluable characteristics in today's law environment, where marketing has only recently become a major focal point for attorneys. Despite practicing for more than four decades, he continues his efforts to expand his client base by working on his practice development plan, displaying a commitment to the kind of effective and strategic marketing that the law firm promotes overall. "The biggest impediment to a great practice is a good practice," he reflects. Thus, in an atmosphere where the best firms are run as businesses rather than boutiques, Rick and his practice are certainly ahead of the curve. His natural warmth is supplemented by a focus on his own ability to promote a sense of humor within himself and his clients that truly lends a unique edge to his outreach. "I've heard that only ten percent of people can remember the jokes they hear," Rick quotes. "I not only remember, but can mentally categorize and recall them at the drop of a hat. One of my partners says that I'm like an old jukebox. Out comes the appropriate record—that is, a joke I can remember—which plays on the turntable and then goes back in its slot."

Rick's current demeanor and warmth warrant even more admiration when compared to his childhood personality, which was decidedly less secure. With a father known for his charm and skills as an in-house general counsel for a Fortune 700 company, Rick was able to model himself after the man's talents while also honing elements of his own unique style. "I remember consciously thinking at age six that I wanted to become an actor," he laughs now. "After that, I always wanted to be a lawyer." He credits his father, then, as the most influential figure in his life, recognizing how he planted a love of law early on that flourished with time.

Thus, in an industry not traditionally known for being lighthearted, Rick's character undoubtedly stands out. "Humor has been a wonderful tool, first and foremost, in putting clients at ease," he reflects. "I've had many clients tell me how much better they feel after talking with me. Frankly, I see this as my job." His impact, then, lies not only in providing exceptional legal advice, but in putting things into perspective for his clients, providing sound practical advice as well. "After practicing for nearly 43 years, I've got enough war stories that I can often reassure my clients about their situations and relieve their anxiety," he explains.

It is clear, then, that Rick has found a true sense of belonging in both his firm and his profession. "The practice of law matches my personality perfectly," he says. "Do lawyers become compulsive people, or do compulsive people become lawyers?" he adds, laughing. Competitive at heart and willing to do virtually anything lawful to achieve success, Rick categorizes himself as the latter—a compulsive person who became a lawyer. Even greater than his commitment to success, however, is Rick's commitment to ethical and just practices, which Lerch, Early, & Brewer strongly promotes overall. "The firm has incredibly high standards of ethics," he describes. "It's great to be in an environment where doing the right thing is expected."

Above and beyond his prominence as a lawyer, however, is Rick's prominence as a family man. Now married to his wife and soul mate of 40 years, he has been blessed with three wonderful children who are now also happily married, two of whom have children of their own. Spending time with family has always been a top priority, and Rick recognizes the monetary sacrifice inherent in maintaining fidelity to such a hierarchy. "The law is a jealous mistress," he points out, "but the opportunity to be a good father and contribute to my children's success has been irreplaceable."

When it comes to advising young entrepreneurs entering the workforce today, Rick's lips are mostly sealed. "I really never gave career advice to my own kids," he remarks. "If I saw a train wreck coming, I'd say something, but for the most part I let them find their own ways." Coming to learn about yourself and developing a clear understanding of what you can and cannot do is a vital step in the process of understanding and appreciating yourself fully, developing a true level of confidence in your own work. "We may be chemically the same, but we are all wired differently," Rick points out. "Recognize who you are, appreciate your strengths, don't overly fault yourself for having flaws, and look to the future, taking it one step at a time." In other words, know what you have so that you, too, can make the best of it.

Michael Weiss

The Most Important Presentation You'll Ever Give

"My company needs to get the word out about something, but I really don't know what we should say about it or how we should do it. Can you help me out with that?"

Words like those are music to Michael Weiss's ears.

As the CEO of Video Labs, Mike's business is presentation. Having essentially built up his professional network and success from scratch through the very art of presentation, he understands that there's nothing more important. He and his team have worked with a wide range of clients, from documentary filmmakers to Capitol Hill politicians, to express and circulate a given message, and there's nothing they love more than drawing on this extensive catalogue of experience to create the perfect product for their clients. "Video Labs's programmers, editors, and graphic designers love the challenge of starting from scratch because they get to do so much more than just fit a widget in a hole; they get to craft a whole board," Mike explains.

Video Labs was founded in April of 1978, but Mike didn't come onboard until June of 2000 when, at the age of 38, he was hired on as COO. Since its inception, the company has ridden the immense waves of technological advancement with a grace that is rare amongst media firms. The company is best described as a media marketing source and began as a firm specializing in making copies of various media items. As the economy has progressed, however, Video Labs has evolved as well. "Today, our business is to help other people communicate their message," Mike explains. "We can help them create that message, or we can take an existing message and disseminate it to the target audience." Thus, the firm is now a blend of public relations, marketing, advertising, and technical work.

Mike's team is now approximately 20 people strong, and their service is so broadly applicable that they have no generic client. "Every business has a message to share with vendors, clients, constituents, what have you," Mike points out. "For example, we might help a business by shooting some footage of their CEO discussing some important information. We can then take that footage, add graphics, put a PowerPoint in there, make copies, and distribute that product out to a million individual people."

Mike grew up in a middle class Jewish family on Long Island in a supportive, loving home, and he credits his parents as the biggest influences in his life. When he was around twelve years old, he asked his father if they were rich, to which he replied, "We're rich in love." No assessment could have been more accurate. Mike remembers the Weiss family as the most stable and encouraging environment one could ask for, and he continues this legacy today with his wife, whom he met in college, and their children. He also infuses this quality into his leadership style at Video Labs, acting as the rock that keeps the company grounded through any storm. "At the top end of the boat, you really need that person who can't be rattled," he points out. "I cultivate a stable environment and reassure people that things are going to be okay."

This calming effect was also evidenced in Mike's role in team sports in his younger years, and it allowed him to foster a great love for athletics. Even at an early age, he was the go-to guy for sports trivia and was an impressive basketball player. He even started writing a book on the topic when he was sixteen. This masterpiece remains unfinished, but he believes that exercise indirectly contributed to his later entrepreneurial success by allowing him to explore the possibility of an endeavor that was wholly self-motivated. He loved the idea of being his own boss and even started a small promotion business with a roommate in college. The entrepreneurial spirit was certainly evident in his attitude and composure, but it would be a while yet before he assembled all the pieces to make the big leap.

Having studied journalism, marketing and public relations, it seemed natural that Mike was engulfed by the media industry from the moment he finished college at the University of Maryland. "I remember having to rush to leave a final exam early because it was my first day of work at ABC News," he laughs. That was May of 1984, and when he showed up for work, a colleague let him know that it was only a six-month temporary position. Mike panicked, having no idea what he would do once the contract was up, but that role manifested itself into a full-time and permanent position before its expiration.

At ABC, he booked satellite feeds, scheduled guests, worked with unions, and was ultimately tasked with scheduling the approximately two hundred engineers needed to fill the different programs of the Washington bureau. Drawing upon his journalism background, he concurrently wrote for ABC's in-house magazine and also did some writing for several other magazines over the years. Life was fast-paced, and Mike was plugged in and working 24 hours a day. "I was very hip to the world, meeting a host of well known figures, but I eventually realized that I wanted to be a bigger fish in a smaller pond," he explains. "I had always wanted to manage a small business, to own something." Thus, with over a decade of experience at ABC under his belt, Mike began to consider striking out on his own.

With his experience and savvy, Mike himself was extremely marketable at the time, but his Achilles heel was networking. "I had gone straight from college to ABC, and I had never really learned the value of networking, or even how to do it," he admits. When he left ABC and realized this gap in his skill set, he hired an outplacement firm to fill it in. The firm taught him how to create contacts by thinking of past employees, friends, family, and acquaintances, and before he knew it, Mike found that he loved the process. "I became a tree," he explains animatedly. "Over a two-year period of time, I made it my second job and committed myself to going out and meeting people to talk, discuss, and discover. It was a great experience—one of the best of my life."

Young entrepreneurs entering the business world today would do well to take a page from Mike's book, and perhaps the most invaluable page would be the one in which that networking flare is underscored. "Every time you meet someone new, you basically have an opportunity to give a presentation about yourself," he points out. "You may have to meet hundreds and hundreds of people before you really master that presentation, but that's okay. It will become the most important presentation you'll ever give, so it's worth it." Mike wrote handwritten thank you letters, built his confidence, and developed a web of contacts that ultimately enabled him to take the leap into realizing his entrepreneurial dreams. He left ABC to work for a handful of other small media firms, achieving General Manager status to the point that he was running them. "That's when I knew I was ready," he concedes. "I was ready to deal with any challenge and ready to go out on my own."

That's when Mike got the call from the owner of Video Labs, who was part of his network. "Mike, I have your resume sitting here," the man had said. "I've got a problem, and I'd like you to come into my office so I can talk with you." Mike had a score of opportunities at his doorstep at the time, but he had an inkling that the position open at Video Labs held the most potential. He accepted it even though other options offered considerably higher compensation. "I knew I wanted to be a business owner somehow, some way, and intuitively I saw that opportunity in Video Labs," he explains. And he was right. In June of 2007, he bought the company.

For Mike, the craft of presentation is truly an art form that he's perfected over the years, and he never would have been able to do so without the very unique and resolute sense of motivation with which he goes through his days. "I don't know how I got this trait, but when I'm motivated, you can't stop me," he avows. "I've never been aggressive, but I am assertive, and if there's something important that I want, I will find that opportunity to succeed." Part of this drive undoubtedly comes from sheer determination—throughout his 27-year career, Mike has only taken 8 sick days, all of which were during his tenure at ABC.

The other part, though, most certainly stems from his life mantra, a Yogi Berra quote that has rung true for him time and again: "It ain't over till it's over." The sports arena boasts countless illustrations of the concept, whether it's the Yankees' unexpected victory in the 1976 World Series or the Islanders' claiming of the Stanley Cup in 1980. Now, Mike refuses to leave a game before the final whistle sounds just as he refuses to admit that Video Labs has had a bad month until all of that month's days have been crossed off the calendar. "Life has just proven to me over and over that you never know how things are going to end," he says. "It's not over till it's over."

When armed with that indelible motivation and that steadfast resolve to see things to the end, young entrepreneurs need only choose the message they want to commit their life to and then focus on presenting it to the world. "There are going to be several times you'll have to dig way down and use that unbelievable motivation to keep you going, but do it," Mike urges. "Things will knock you down along the way, but stay on track and don't forget who you are and what you want." Your message will certainly evolve over the years, and your audience will undoubtedly shift as time goes on, but remembering that your presentation "ain't over till it's over" in this way means that there's always time to make it stronger, sweeter, and more your own.

Armando Ygbuhay

Much Ventured, Much Gained

When Armando Ygbuhay first learned about HCI|integrated solutions (HCI) in 2004, although not entirely impressed, he knew the company had the potential to be a lot more. First launched in 1995, the company had achieved moderate success in its first decade. Acting primarily as a seller and reseller of technology products, it was drawing $250 thousand in revenue at most any given year. "To be frank, the business was not the most attractive deal for most folks," Armando recalls. "They only had a few contracts and had limited options for growth at the time, so I knew the endeavor was a risk, but I decided that it was a risk I was willing to take. I was interested in what I could do with it and in the potential gains associated with it." It is often said that nothing is gained if nothing is ventured, and Armando decided to venture quite a bit.

He first got involved as an equity position and assumed the role of President and CEO after HCI's original owners had a falling out with his partners. Then one of those owners passed away within a year of Armando's arrival. Distraught yet determined to guide the company to new success, he restructured the organization, assuming the majority ownership. He moved the headquarters from Florida to Fairfax, Virginia, and broadened HCI's horizons by expanding into the services realm and focusing on the Federal marketplace, taking on the Department of Defense as its primary client. Things were changing drastically for the small company, but it appears Armando knew what he was doing. Within a year of this transformation, he had grown the company to $2 million in revenue. Then, in the five years that followed, that figure escalated to a staggering $25 million, and HCI now boasts a work force of over 270 employees worldwide. Today, the professional services firm provides information technology, training, and logistics support as their core services, delivering quality staffing and technology support to the Federal government on a global scale.

Armando had spent only five years working in the corporate world prior to his involvement with HCI, but this is not to say that he was not an expert in the firm's subject matter. Growing up in a home of modest means in a small town in Ohio, he had always held jobs, working a morning and afternoon paper route and then stocking shelves in the local grocery store. "I was always accustomed to working, and when the store closed down, there weren't many jobs to be had around there," he remembers. "So, driven by circumstance and ethic to work, I joined the army at age 17."

In a sense, being in the military is about orienting one's self toward the future. "In basic training, a large part of the indoctrination process revolves around succeeding and winning," Armando explains. "What else is there?" Ingrained with this progressive attitude at an early age, he found himself constantly driven to seek out the life tales of older military personnel—those who had already retired or who were facing retirement. He was fascinated by their stories, finding invaluable life lessons woven between the words that he incorporated into his own system of discipline and planning. "Some of the stories were good, while others were bad, and I tailored their lessons into where I wanted to go and what I wanted to do," he says. "It was an almost academic pursuit to learn through the experiences of others. You don't know what you don't know, you know?" he adds with a laugh.

Armando's military career spanned twenty years, and in that time he forged an extensive network of invaluable contacts and an unrivaled expertise in the field. When his second decade of service came to a close, he submitted his retirement paperwork with confidence, unsure of the exact path his future would take but certain that it would be a good one. He had several job offers in the DC metro area, so he made the cross-continental move from the state of Washington, beginning his new career within a week of the transition.

"The military was all I had ever known, but I had always been fascinated by the corporate world," says Armando. He accepted a position with AT&T initially as a Subject Matter Expert and later transitioning into the role of project manager for several government contracts. The company had recently acquired GRC International, which was to comprise its Federal services branch. The initiative was not without its growing pains, but Armando appreciated the experience, only deciding to leave after AT&T was purchased by SBC. "I realized that, if I was going to go through an organizational change like that, why not just go out on my own?" he recalls. "I had always considered pursuing my entrepreneurial drive, and the acquisition of AT&T set things in motion organically."

Interestingly enough yet unsurprising in light of his character, Armando's involvement with HCI has never been about money. Rather, it was about taking those life lessons he had absorbed and applying them in strategic and effective ways to achieve success where few would dare to try. "I was most driven by the challenge of making this company great," he explains. "As the President and CEO, I had direct control over the risk I was taking and felt comfortable about that risk."

A strategist by nature, Armando recognized early on that it would be difficult for a professional services company to differentiate itself from the competition based on quantity. Thus, HCI instead focuses on quality. "We really take the time to invest in finding the most qualified and skilled individuals for our clients' staffing needs," he says. The company pursues skill sets primarily focused in logistics and maintenance supporting facilities services, which makes up about seventy percent of its business. "That's my background, and that's the marketplace I know best," Armando confirms.

Despite the notoriously tough environment of our nation's military, Armando maintains that bringing the company to where it is today has been his greatest challenge, and guiding it toward even greater success promises to be his greatest challenge in the future. Indeed, HCI has enjoyed small business success and has been able to capitalize on the opportunities that have come its way so far, but Armando has his sights set on taking the enterprise to the next level. "We're well on our way to achieving a large business status, and I don't want to be one of those companies that falls back into the small business realm," he explains. "In all things and in all aspects of life, I am firmly committed to moving only forward, never backward. Because going backward is simply not an option for us, what does the future look like? This is what I am exploring now."

A performance oriented company, HCI's motto is *Make it Happen*, and it employs this motto as it progresses steadily toward Armando's vision. HCI measures this performance through consistency and completion of projects, and Armando maintains a leadership style that demands excellence. His primary role at this point in the organization's development is the establishment of an infrastructure that supports the growth of the company, while also focusing on driving that growth through business development initiatives.

Make it Happen. It's a motto that hearkens back to Armando's military days when he had his hands inside nuclear bombs. Working with nuclear components demanded more from the soundness of his psychology than it did from the dexterity of his hands. It's the motto that he lived by in fostering strong relationships with his children, whose childhoods were largely lacking in the immediate presence of their father due to the aftermath of divorce and the stark realities of being stationed in different parts of the country. "I'm a firm believer that you have to turn bad experiences into good experiences," Armando avows. "Make lemonade out of lemons. If someone thinks ill of you, consider it a challenge and an honor to prove them wrong."

By employing this philosophy, Armando is able to see life's adversity and challenges through a unique lens—one that views each difficult encounter as the kind of growing experience that living is all about. "There's always room for improvement, and embracing challenge rather than running from it is the key to unlocking those opportunities" he points out. "With this in mind, I run HCI by setting the bar high, achieving those goals, and then setting the bar higher. We're about perpetual growth, so we're always looking for that next level."

In advising young entrepreneurs entering the workforce today, Armando echoes the importance of this pursuit of opportunity, as life-changing moments can be hidden in even the most obscure of experiences. "Life is all about timing and putting yourself in a position to capitalize on opportunities," he emphasizes. Armando himself, for instance, joined the military after the unexpected setback of losing his job, yet he considers this move to be among the best decisions of his life. Had he resigned to the discouragement of the immediate moment rather than orienting himself toward the future and pursuing new thresholds, he could never have become the leader he is today.

Beyond this, it comes as little surprise that he also stresses the importance of learning from those around you. "Everyone has a history," says Armando. "Though you may be starting from the beginning, you don't have to start with nothing. Use the stories of those around you to turn yours into a great one." When one understands that the wrong answers can hold just as much value as the right answers and that hardship is often the vehicle through which true strength of character is composed, life's challenges become not only necessary, but welcome.

Andrew Zeinfeld

The Win-Win-Win-Win Situation

The very best businesses are those that can seemingly create something out of nothing, providing customers with such cost-effective and quality products that they're left to wonder how the company manages to make a profit. In essence, they are the win-win situations—those in which both the client and the company are delighted by the outcome. Some companies even take it a step further, creating win-win-win situations where a third party benefits as well—a manufacturer, for instance. But one company even surpasses this ideal, bringing forth the win-win-win-win experience.

It is amusing that, while most businesses prohibit the use of Facebook and other social media sites at work, this win-win-win-win company actually embraces it. Andy Zeinfeld, however, considers these modern networking tools an imperative part of his workday. As the CEO of Simplexity, one of the leading wireless retailers in the country and the largest online American retailer of wireless devices, Andy leverages these sites to analyze up-to-the-minute feedback from customers. The fact that he monitors such online venues each morning and evening is just one of many examples in which Simplexity has harnessed the power of the modern internet community and used it to transform the way we conceptualize of business today.

Simplexity was formed when the assets of InPhonic, Inc, a company founded in 1997 that filed for bankruptcy in 2007, were purchased. As part of that transaction, Simplexity acquired Wirefly.com, a site where customers can easily compare cell phones and rate plans across carriers to select the purchase that's best for them, and at a fraction of the cost. Wirefly customers often pay $50 to $200 less than they would in a retail store. A hot-off-the-presses Android-powered smartphone selling in the store for $225 with a $100 rebate, for example, might very well sell on Wirefly for free and without the hassle of rebates. The dramatic price reductions are made possible by the fact that Wirefly is internet-based, which keeps company costs substantially lower than those of traditional bricks-and-mortar venues. When a consumer buys and activates a phone through Wirefly, the carrier, in turn, pays a commission to Simplexity for acquiring a new customer for them. The consumer is thus paying for the same coverage and the same customer service they would get when buying directly from the carrier, but does not shoulder the burden of the retail store, salespeople, and advertising expenses. It's a win for the customer, a win for the carrier, and a win for Simplexity.

Simplexity also builds and operates private-labeled websites to sell wireless products and services for some of the most recognized brands in the world, including RadioShack, Sears, Kmart, Dell, HP, Target, TigerDirect, and Newegg, in return for a commission. Its proprietary e-commerce platform offers technology solutions that include online merchandising, rate plan management, procurement, high-level customer care and customer relationship marketing, billing, order processing, automated cell phone activations and fulfillment. These big name retailers partner with Simplexity to leverage its infrastructure so they don't have to invest money to build a costly system to sell phones. As a result, both Simplexity and the retailers receive a pure profit for every customer that purchases a phone via their websites. Thus, the definitive fourth win is added to the equaion.

One fatal flaw of InPhonic's business model and strategy was its focus on top-line growth and, therefore, the lack of focus and selectivity in its customer base. If an individual received a free phone and then neglected to pay their monthly bill to the carrier, it could cost InPhonic up to $400 for the loss of the equipment and of the commission from the carrier. To remedy this, Andy now insists that Simplexity runs fraud checks and credit score reviews on every customer before approving an order and shipping a phone.

The other Achilles' heel of InPhonic was its preoccupation with hyper top line revenue. "Having top line growth is great," Andy concedes, "but you have to have bottom line profitability to support it." InPhonic excelled at selling its product, but it constantly did so at a loss. This mistake was perpetuated by a weak alignment between growth and expenses. "You cannot allow expenses to outpace growth, and vice versa," says Andy.

Thus, when Andy first joined InPhonic in 2006 as President of E-Commerce, he could tell instantly that he had his work cut out for him. "My job wasn't in Profit & Loss or Finance, but I could see the writing on the wall," he reflects. When he stepped up to the plate as CEO toward the end of 2007, he could discern within the first thirty days that InPhonic had made itself the brunt of a win-win-win-lose situation. Confronting the challenge of declaring bankruptcy, he organized a conference call before sending the news public and invited each employee to participate. "My job is to build a future business," he told them, "one you and your families can be proud of; one in which you can feel secure that you'll have a career and a paycheck week to week." If anything has been driving his work ethic and dedication since that day, it has been this promise.

At this point, Andy met with representatives from Versa Capital Management, a private equity firm that invests in companies where it identifies real potential in the business model. Along with his management team, Andy pinpointed the exact obstacles InPhonic faced and the specific steps needed to overcome them. Versa knew value when they saw it and quickly bought the assets of the company, thus ending the dog days of InPhonic and launching a new era with Simplexity. The power inherent in the basic business model has remained intact since the transition, but the overall execution, management, and quality control have changed drastically.

This comes as no surprise when one considers the brand of leadership that Andy employs. Above all else, he is uncompromisingly committed to detail-oriented execution. "I believe in dotting the i's and crossing the t's," he says. "It's all in the details." Associates often advise that he shouldn't be involved at that level, but he argues it's just the opposite. "I'm the CEO of the company, and therefore *every* detail means something to me."

This acute level of specificity parallels the work ethic of Andy's father, who is known to compute numbers in his head faster than many people can punch them into a calculator. The man, who owned harness race horses, would arrive at the stable early each morning to watch them train and would then stay late through the evening to watch them race. He would thoroughly analyze the competition as well as his own strong and weak points, and his knowledge of which horses to pick, breed, buy, and sell was unmatched in the industry. A business orientation permeated both his professional and personal demeanor, and he often shared the concepts behind the numbers with his son. "Both of us only know how to do things one way: all the way, or not at all," Andy explains. "There is no part-time. I think people are either wired this way, or they aren't."

With his father racing horses throughout the country, it was not unusual for the family to move three or four times a year. Once the constant uproot became too much, they settled in California, where

Andy applied his excellent work ethic to his first job as a part-time salesperson at RadioShack in 1979. Making $1.95 an hour plus commission, he adored the experience so much that he stayed with the company for the next twenty-eight years. He did not pursue a college education, but this was irrelevant to his success. "Working there was the best college education and the best MBA program you could find," he confirms. Quickly moving up the ranks from store manager, to district manager, to more senior executive level positions, and eventually to Chief Retail Officer for the entire corporation, Andy loved to assume leadership in the worst markets because he knew he could turn them around—a skill echoed in his later success with Simplexity.

Ever since he first received a sales call at RadioShack from an InPhonic representative, he thought the business model was ingenious. Not only could InPhonic help RadioShack by handling its website, but it had so much potential. "I had a vision of it being replicated over and over again, leveraging infrastructure like RadioShack did," says Andy. He built close ties with InPhonic's CEO, who often discussed Andy coming to work for the company. Andy, however, remained hesitant, as he had always pictured his future with RadioShack. Then, by a serendipitous turn of events, he was vacationing with his wife two years later on a small island off of Florida when he heard someone call his name from down the beach. With less than two hundred people inhabiting the region, he was incredulous to find InPhonic's CEO waltzing toward him and took it as an omen, finally resigning from his position as Chief Retail Services Officer, which oversaw a division he himself had built from scratch and ultimately grown to two thousand employees.

"Looking back at it, I'm one of the luckiest guys that's ever been around," he concedes. "I've built relationships with some pretty fantastic people." In fact, many of the skills behind his success—the power of cash flow, the ability to mine for answers, the nuance of customer service—are directly linked to the people that populate his personal history. The former CEO of RadioShack, Len Roberts, for instance, taught him how to work effectively with people and about the importance of managing with two ears and one mouth—in other words, the most effective leaders listen twice as much as they speak. Andy values these individuals not only as business partners, but also as friends. His genuine fascination with and affection for humanity has not only enriched his life, but has also made him the incredible success story that he is today. His greatest piece of advice to young entrepreneurs, then, is essentially to be a human sponge. "You can learn something from everybody," he urges. "Even the person you dislike the most will teach you something good, so you have to listen."

Of Simplexity's future, Andy is unwaveringly optimistic, and with good reason. "We've got an oyster here," he marvels. "There's no telling how big or successful this company can be." The true basis for this confidence is the fact that the company's tremendous growth and success thus far have come despite its relative obscurity. Because they haven't invested the billions of dollars in marketing that many of their contemporaries have, Simplexity and Wirefly.com are relative unknown. When they fully invest in building the brand to lock down top-of-mind awareness, returns promise to escalate accordingly.

Not only does its business model make for such potential, but also the industry itself boasts tremendous opportunity. With connectivity and technology growing at what seems an exponential rate in terms of capability, breadth, and prominence, Simplexity is privy to an ever-expanding product base. Today, Andy expresses interest in leveraging this power to expand the company internationally. "We're lucky," he says. "We're at the right place at the right time." Without a doubt, Andy will continue to help Simplexity win-win-win-win for many years to come.

About the Author

Having grown up on a farm in Nebraska, Gordon Bernhardt left the Midwest in the early 1980s for Washington D.C. to work as an assistant in the U.S. House of Representatives. He left behind the rural lifestyle but he carried with him the values of hard work, a focus on what you can control, and service to others—values that continue to influence his life, today.

After completing a bachelor's degree in Commerce at the University of Virginia, Bernhardt began a successful career in finance at a leading accounting firm and two different brokerage companies. In 1994, in order to make the kind of difference in people's lives that he hoped to make, he established Bernhardt Wealth Management, an independent registered investment advisory firm built on the principle of fiduciary care: providing investment and wealth management guidance, service, and advice that places clients' interests and needs ahead of everything else. By adhering to this higher standard, he removed the conflicts of interest that were prevalent elsewhere. Rather than be restricted by a large company's cookie cutter methodology, he and his team are able to create customized plans that are far more appropriate for individual clients. Today, Bernhardt Wealth Management is recognized as one of the top fee-only wealth management firms in the Washington D.C. region.

In addition to being an entrepreneur and wealth manager, Bernhardt is the author of *Buen Camino: What a Hike through Spain Taught Me about Investing and Life*, a memoir about the 35-day, 618-mile pilgrimage he completed in Spain and the lessons he learned along the way. He also writes a weekly finance blog. Bernhardt writes the *Profiles in Success: Inspiration from Executive Leaders* book series, and hosts a podcast with the same name, to expand the influence of outstanding leaders while inspiring the next generation of executives.

Find out more about Gordon Bernhardt at
www.BernhardtWealth.com and www.ProfilesInSuccess.com.

Pvt. Jonathan Lee Gifford was the first U.S. soldier killed in Iraq. He was killed just two days into the war on March 23, 2003. Spc. David Emanual Hickman was killed by a roadside bomb in Iraq on November 14, 2011. *The Washington Post* on December 17, 2011, said Hickman "may have been the last" U.S. soldier killed in Iraq. After reading an article about Gifford and Hickman my sister, Gloria, was inspired to write the following poem.

From Gifford to Hickman

by Gloria J. Bernhardt

From Gifford to Hickman…and all those in between,
You fought bravely amid chaos and dangers unforeseen.
Twenty-one guns have sounded, the riderless horse walks on.
Fond memories are remaining. A nation's child is gone.

Sons and daughters; fathers, mothers—broken hearts intertwined.
Hugs and kisses; their successes—major milestones left behind.
Your selfless gift—a life laid down; for fellow soldier, family, land.
Duty called—call was answered—no greater love hath man.

"I'm getting taller. I lost a tooth. I got 100 on my test!
Miss your pancakes and your tickles, goodnight kisses were the best.
Who will answer all my questions now? I've important stuff to learn!
You said you had a big surprise on the day that you'd return."

"I talk to you at bedtime—after lights go out at night.
I told Jesus that I miss you…sure wish you could hug me tight.
When Grandpa says I look like you, Grandma starts to cry.
I'm mad that you're not coming home…I need to say goodbye!"

From Gifford, to Hickman, through every soldier who has served,
Liberty's fruits are savored and freedom is preserved.
We live freely due to soldiers, willing to support and defend
Our Constitution, our country—against enemies 'til the end.

Sons and daughters; fathers, mothers—broken hearts intertwined.
Hugs and kisses; their successes—major milestones left behind.
Your selfless gift—a life laid down; for fellow soldier, family, land.
Duty called—call was answered—no greater love hath man.

"I had a dream the night before…you smiled and walked on by.
When I awoke, I thought it odd…it seemed like a 'good-bye'.
I couldn't put my finger on the dark cloud that remained,
When the phone began to ring…I knew my life had changed."

"I questioned God, 'Why MY child? Why do I have to lose?'
I imagined His response would be 'If not your child, then whose?'
Your bright life flashed too briefly… seems He only takes the best.
I'm thankful for the time I had. For that I'm truly blessed."

From Gifford to Hickman and every warrior who has passed,
The price you've paid bought freedom, but will we make it last?
Your last breath drawn for citizens in this country and abroad
Are we worthy of such gifts is known only but to God.

Sons and daughters; fathers, mothers—broken hearts intertwined.
Hugs and kisses; their successes—major milestones left behind.
Your selfless gift—a life laid down; for fellow soldier, family, land.
Duty called—call was answered—no greater love hath man.

"My world stopped spinning…I couldn't breathe! Lord, how can I go on?
My days are all one midnight…but they say it's darkest 'fore the dawn.
I can hear you say, 'I'm proud of you! I know that this is hard.'
What do I do without you here? What dreams do I discard?"

"I miss your laugh. I miss your smell. I even miss our fights.
No more messes. No embraces. It's more 'real' late at night.
I saw you in a crowd today; but you vanished in the throng.
Wishful thinking changes nothing! I know my "rock" is gone."

FOR Gifford, FOR Hickman…FOR all the fallen in between,
You've trudged through shadowed valley and joined heroes' ranks unseen.
Upon freedom's altar, we sacrificed our daughters and our sons.
Empty boots stand at attention. The flag is folded. Your mission's done.

BERNHARDT

WEALTH MANAGEMENT

Made in United States
Orlando, FL
04 November 2026

90200499R00154